The Notables of Cuddington Sandiway and Delamere Park

by JILL E. KING

The Author

Jill King was born at her maternal grandparents' home in the idyllic estate village of Edensor in Chatsworth Park, Derbyshire. The family spent a short time in Great Budworth before settling in Cuddington in 1951, Jill's father being employed at William Horner's Creamery, the subject of her first book. Local historical research has become a passion for Jill since her retirement from the teaching profession. This latest offering takes a look at the lives of village residents, past and present, who have made exceptional contributions that have impacted beyond the immediate Mid-Cheshire locality.

First published in the United Kingdom in 2016
by C.C.Publishing (Chester)
Martins Lane, Hargrave, Chester, CH3 7RX
http://www.cc-publishing.co.uk

Copyright © Jill E. King, 2016

The right of Jill E. King to be identified as the author of this work has been asserted by her in accordance with the Copyright, Designs and Patents Act, 1988. All rights reserved. No part of this book may be reproduced or transmitted in any form or by any means, electronic or mechanical, including photocopying, recording or otherwise without the prior permission in writing of the copyright holder, nor be otherwise circulated in any form or binding or cover other than in which it is published and without a similar condition being imposed on the subsequent publisher.

ISBN: 978-0-949001-57-3

INTRODUCTION

The life of each Cuddington and Sandiway resident, past and present, is unique and all have an interesting story to tell, but the aim of this book is to bring together the men and women from our village who have achieved something truly exceptional. All those listed have gained renown outside their locality, some nationally, a handful internationally. On occasions it has been necessary to include several members of one family and, though only accidents of birth, it has not been possible to ignore inherited titles and wealth. Probate details up to 1966 are in the public domain, so where appropriate, and particularly if that person reached millionaire status, they have been included. Where historically sums of money are mentioned, its approximate value in 2016 follows in brackets.

Lancashire was the birthplace of the Industrial Revolution and by the 1830s approximately 85% of all cotton was manufactured in the county. Manchester and Liverpool grew quickly, both dominating global trade, but soon the surrounding towns started to follow suit and by the 1870s the county encompassed several hundred mill towns. Many cotton merchants and men with factories associated with the textile industry, made massive fortunes and then decided to escape the grime and gloom. A fair number chose the rural tranquillity of Cuddington and Sandiway with it's easy train access to the big cities and close proximity to fox hunting, a popular pastime of the day. Close on thirty grand, country houses were built in the village and these fine dwellings have continued to lure gentry, wealthy businessmen and well known celebrities, right up to the present day. However, it is a sad fact that in the past, this wealth, made as it so often was on the back of cotton, was linked to the institution of slavery.

For the most part the Cuddington and Sandiway Parish boundary has been adhered to. Gorstage and Speedwell have been treated as part of the village, and one section is devoted to a dozen or so personalities who have warranted a short excursion over the permitted line. Literature, Mathematics, Science, Music, Sport, the Creative Arts, Architecture, the Military, Industry and Politics: all are within. Research has uncovered some surprising facts and interesting characters. With some exceptions these eminent residents have been organised in alphabetical order with three groups of villagers at the end of the book under the headings: More Millionaires, The Tarporley-Hunt and The Must Mentions.

Thank you to all those who have sent me photographs and information to help in my research. It has been such a pleasure to be in touch with so many new people but I am particularly grateful to Roger King, Mark Bevan, Bronwen Hawke and Nichola Forbes (for the Hawke family information), Mary Riley (for Dominic Riley), Blanche Westbrook (Lord Hinton), Jennifer Garner (William Garner and Pamela Clarkson), Margaret Sherry (for herself and Tom Sherry) and Julie Summers. I hope everyone enjoys reading it.

Jill E. King

HERBERT and RICHARD ASHTON

1797 - 1876 and 1799 - 1867

Herbert Ashton lived at Sandiway Lodge, and Richard Ashton, Gorstage Hall. They were the second and youngest of three sons born to John Ashton and Mary Noble Jarrett of Hefferston Grange, Weaverham. Their first child, also named John, was killed at the battle of Waterloo in 1815, and there is a memorial to his memory in St Mary's Church, Weaverham.

Gorstage Hall today.

The Ashton family were amongst the richest entrepreneurs in the Northwest; much of their immense wealth was founded in the African slave trade. Richard and Herbert's Grandfather and Great grandfather, Nicholas and John Ashton, were involved in the development of communications from the Cheshire and Lancashire salt and coal fields to the River Mersey and Liverpool. Nicholas Ashton, a Magistrate and High Sheriff of Lancashire at the time, bought the impressive Woolton Hall, set on a 400 acre estate in Liverpool and leased coal mines in Parr and St Helens. He also purchased Dunkirk, a major salt works in Northwich, Hefferston Grange, and 200 acres in Cuddington, Gorstage, and along the River Weaver at Acton Bridge. Opened in 1757, John was one of the principal designers and financiers of the Sankey Canal, the first canal of the British Industrial Revolution. He also owned the Dungeon Salt Works, at Hale Head, on the foreshore of the Mersey.

Nicholas Ashton, the grandfather of Herbert and Richard Aston.

Built by Herbert Ashton, Sandiway Lodge is now a nursing home for the elderly.

Nicholas and his wife, Mary Philpot (page 120), had eight children and it was their eldest, John, who was the father of Herbert and Richard. On John's death, in 1833, Herbert inherited most of the family fortune but couldn't live at Hefferston as it had been leased, for life, to Lady Brooke, so he built Sandiway Lodge for himself and Gorstage Hall (set in forty acres) for his younger brother, Richard.

On 14th April 1809, when he was just eleven, Herbert Ashton had joined the Royal Navy and served on the 74-gun *HMS Implacable,* stationed in the Baltic, under Captain Byam Martin. There followed spells with the warships: the *Surveillante (38-gun), Centaur (74), Sybille (44)* and *Leander (50).* He was promoted to Lieutenant, on 20th September 1815, after witnessing the destruction of the French, 74-gun ship, *Regulus*; three brigs of war and several smaller vessels, near Bordeaux. Herbert married twice, both times to French ladies, Heloise Clement and Marie Perron Usannaz. He spent much of his life abroad and was buried in Nice.

Two bricks bearing the R. ASHTON & CO. stamp.

Richard Ashton's life took a very different course to that of his brother. Although born in Portland Place, London, he was baptised in Weaverham and educated in Winchester. In March 1841 he bought the Knowle Lane brickworks in Buckley, Mold. Many types of brick and pieces of tile and pot, bearing the R. Ashton and Co. stamp, have been unearthed in and around Flintshire and even as far as Northern Ireland. The 1851 and 1861 censuses record that Richard was a "landed proprietor" living in lavish style in Gorstage Hall with a host of "servants" and "employing seventy men" - presumably at his works. In 1850 he married Louisa, the third daughter of Sir John L. Lister-Kaye of Derby Grange, Yorkshire. Gorstage Hall was their home for the rest of their lives. After Richard's death the business was leased, by Louisa, to two brothers, Frederick and Richard Prince, who continued trading under the Ashton name. Frederick had been Richard Ashton's manager.

When Louisa Ashton died in 1872, she left £14,000 (£1.1m) to her sole surviving heir, her nephew, Edward John Ward of Appleby Castle, Westmorland. Both Richard and Louisa Ashton are buried in St Mary's Churchyard, Weaverham. The brickworks ceased trading in 1902.

Industrial Scene - a painting by James Bentley which is held by the Buckley Library, Museum and Gallery. It is a view which Richard Ashton would have seen each day. There were 25 brickworks in and around Buckley and Richard's was one of the earliest, dating from the 1790s. Knowle Lane is the fifth chimney along from the left.

RICHARD "DICK" ALFORD BANKS

1902 - 1997

Richard Alford Banks lived at The Mount, Cuddington (page 92). He had two successful careers, first as an industrialist at ICI, and then as a noted gardener. Dick Banks, as he was known, is best remembered for his development of the seventy-acre Herefordshire garden at Hergest Croft, begun by his father towards the end of the nineteenth century. It is now one of England's great woodland gardens, attracting around 13,000 visitors each year. At Hergest, Dick Banks developed one of the finest collections of trees and shrubs in the country, with several thousand species and forms, many of great rarity. Some sixty of the mature trees have been registered as British champions for their size, and three National Collections: maple, birch and zelkova (a species of the elm family) are held there.

Richard Alford Banks
Painting by Robert Tolhurst.

Richard Alford Banks was born into a family of country lawyers and bankers at Kington, Herefordshire, where his ancestors had lived for three generations. In 1926 he went to India to study opportunities for the exploitation of soda in industrial processes. Dick made his home in Cuddington when he became involved in the production of polythene at ICI, Winnington. Polythene was an ICI patent, discovered there accidentally in the 1930s. He was managing director of its Alkali division and in 1952 was appointed to the ICI board of directors.

On retirement from ICI, in 1963, Dick Banks devoted himself to the family estate. During the war, the house at Hergest Croft had been requisitioned so he built himself a log cabin in the grounds, from which he directed reclamation of the huge woodland from its recent neglect. In spite of the great area his garden covered, and the range of species grown there, Dick knew all the plants intimately and always protested that he was not an estate owner but "a hands-on gardener". In 1983, The Royal Horticultural Society acknowledged his contribution to horticulture with the award of the Veitch Memorial Medal.

In 1936 Dick Banks married Lillian Jean Walker who died in 1974; they had two sons and a daughter. In 1976, he wed Rosamund Gould. His oldest son, Lawrence, who was born in 1938 at The Mount, took over the stewardship of the garden in 1988 and has continued to enrich the plantings. He was awarded a CBE for his services to banking and was a former treasurer of the Royal Horticultural Society. His wife, Elizabeth, is a highly successful landscape artist and was elected as the first female President of the RHS in 2011.

GARY BARLOW

b. 1971

Gary Barlow is probably the most famous of all Cuddington and Sandiway residents. He lived at Delamere Manor from 1995 until 2005 when the mansion was sold for seven and a half million pounds. Gary has gained international stardom as a singer-songwriter, pianist, composer and record producer. He is one of Britain's most successful songwriters, having written 14 Number One singles and 24 Top Ten hits. As a solo artist, he has had three Number One and six Top Ten singles and two Number One albums. Gary is a six-time recipient of the Ivor Novello Award and has sold over fifty million records worldwide. In 2012 he was presented with an OBE for services to music and charity. He has raised millions for charities such as Children in Need, Comic Relief, Barnados, Help for Heroes, The Princes Trust, and his concerts always require the largest arenas: tickets are soon sold out. He is front man and lead vocalist of the British pop-group Take That with whom he has achieved 17 top five hits, twelve Number One singles and seven Number One albums. He served as head judge on series eight, nine and ten of the talent show, *The X Factor UK*.

Gary Barlow
Photo: Matt Deegan

Gary Barlow was born, on the 20th January 1971, in Frodsham, to Colin and Marjorie Barlow. In his autobiography, he relates that his love of music began at an early age. He says, "I was one of those kids that's forever dancing in front of the TV looking at my reflection." In 2000, Gary married Dawn Andrews, who was a dancer on their 1995, *Nobody Else* tour. They have three children: Daniel (born 2000), Emily (2002), and Daisy (2009). In 2012, their fourth child, Poppy, was stillborn. Gary has one sibling, a brother Ian, who is a builder and lives in Cuddington with his wife, Lisa, and their three children

Delamere Manor

At the beginning of May 2010, it was announced that Queen Elizabeth had asked Gary to organise her 86th birthday party, and in 2012, the celebrations for her Diamond Jubilee. A source said, "Her Majesty has been made well aware of his charity work and the events he has put together. She knows that Gary has got the power to pull in the big names across the music industry and to ensure it's a party to match the occasion." In the Summer of 2012 Gary Barlow sang *Rule the World* at the closing Ceremony of the London Olympics games.

He credits Elton John as inspiring him to play the piano and, indeed, Elton was a frequent visitor to Delamere Manor, as were Donny Osmond and the R & B band, Blue. Fans came from afar to sit outside Gary's imposing iron gates, hoping to spot any well known visitors or get a glimpse of the star himself. His spectacular firework displays, on November 5th, lit up the sky over the surrounding villages and were the talk of the locality for days to come.

WILLIAM BATTERSBY

1860 - 1923

Lymm Hall, family seat of the Battersbys.

William Battersby Sr.

Sarah Emmeline Hartridge, William Battersby's mother.

According to the 1891 census, by the age of 31, William Battersby was "living on his own means" at Pemberton Cottage, Norley Road, Sandiway, with his sister, Sarah Dorcas Battersby (soon to be Mrs Faulkner), and "four servants", including a "waitress". Their father, William Battersby Sr, had been one of the most successful cotton merchants of the American South, living most of his working life in Savannah, Georgia. In 1850, he built a handsome West Indian style brick house on 119, East Charlton Street, and it is here that his five children - William, and his four sisters: Josephine, Emmeline, Sarah and Mary were born. The striking dwelling features a shuttered balcony facing a "walled antebellum parterre" garden said to be one of the few surviving gardens of its type. It involves symmetrical, formal patterns of planted beds edged with clipped boxwood and gravel.

The Battersby country residence in England was Lymm Hall, Cheshire, where William senior returned in about 1868. He died there in 1883. Two stained glass windows were installed in St Mary's Church, Lymm, one in memory of William Battersby Sr and his daughter Mary, who passed away when only in her thirties, and the other for Sarah Dorcas Faulkner, William Battersby's sister. William Battersby died in 1923 at Kempsford Manor, Gloucestershire. He never married but left £98,293 (nearly £5m). In 1926 a £1,000 (£55,000) trust for the poor was set up in Kempsford in memory of William Battersby and, even today, the village primary school divide their pupils into four houses of which one is named Battersby. William Battersby lived at The Manor, which was owned by his brother-in-law, William Faulkner, for over twenty years.

Left - Hartridge House, Savannah, built by William Battersby Sr and the birthplace of all his children.
Right - Pemberton Cottage, as it is today - now Portobello, its name according to Bryant's map of 1831 and the 1875 OS map. The foundation stone over the door dates the dwelling to 1777.

KEITH RICHARD BEBBINGTON

b. 1943

Keith Richard Bebbington is a former English footballer who played in the Football League for Stoke City, Oldham Athletic and Rochdale. In total he made 398 appearances for these clubs and scored 62 goals.

The son of Arthur and Nancy Bebbington, Keith was born in Pinfold Hollows, Cuddington, on 4th August 1943 and has lived in the village for much of his life. He has a wife, Gill, and three children: Mark, Daniel and Sarah.

Keith Richard Bebbington

Keith Bebbington was a speedy left winger who came through the youth team at Stoke City and made his debut against Luton Town in September 1962, in place of the legendary Stanley Matthews. He had a good first season with Stoke as they won the Second Division title. In 1963-1964 Stoke made it to the 1964 Football League Cup Final against Leicester City and Keith scored the first goal of a two legged tie, becoming Stoke's first cup final goal scorer. Unfortunately they lost 4–3 on aggregate.

In the 1965-1966 season the "substitute rule" was introduced and Bebbington was Stoke's first "sub" replacing Dennis Viollet on the opening day, away at Arsenal. He spent two more seasons at Stoke's Victoria Ground, and after making 124 appearances and scoring 22 goals, left for Oldham Athletic where he was a key player for the club, with 237 league appearances in six years and 39 goals.

Keith Bebbington finished his career with Rochdale, from 1972 until 1974.

Keith playing away for Stoke City against Wolves in the 1963 - 1964 season. The year before Stoke City were the Second Division Champions. During this period Keith played alongside such famous names, in football, as Eddie Clamp, Bill Asprey, Jimmy O'Neill, Tony Allen, Stanley Matthews, Dennis Viollet, Eddie Stuart, Jackie Mudie, Jimmy McIlroy, Don Ratcliffe and Eric Skeels.

HENRY "HARRY" BEECHAM

1888 - 1947

It was during WWI that Henry Beecham, the younger brother of Sir Thomas Beecham, the internationally renowned conductor and impresario, made his home at Forest Hill House in Sandiway (page 102). This splendid residence has magnificent views over Sandiway Golf Course and the neighbouring countryside. Henry was born in another large dwelling named Evansville, in Huyton, Liverpool. His mother, Josephine Burnett, married Sir Joseph Beecham 1st Baronet, the son of Thomas Beecham, of Beecham's Powder fame. They had eight children and Joseph bequeathed to his family the unbelievable sum, in today's money, of over £77.7 million. In 1911, when Henry was 22, he worked as a "wholesale druggist manufacturer of patent medicines", presumably in his grandfather's firm.

In 1914, Henry married Ethel Anne Baxter. They had five children: (Helen) Audrey (born 1915), Major Joseph Michael Beecham MBE (1917), Henry (1921), Paul (1923) and Christopher (1925). Helen and Joseph were born at Forest Hill, but the venue for the other three is uncertain. Ethel Beecham died in 1956, aged 61.

The only daughter of Henry Beecham, (Helen) Audrey Beecham - poet, writer and lecturer at Nottingham University.
Painting by Tony Cowlishaw.

Sir Joseph Beecham had agreed, in July 1914, to buy the Covent Garden estate from the Duke of Bedford. The deal was described by *The Times* as "one of the largest ever carried out in real estate in London". However, in October 1916, Joseph Beecham died suddenly, with the transaction incomplete. The matter was brought before the civil courts with the aim of disentangling Sir Joseph's affairs. In order to complete the Covent Garden contract the court and all parties agreed that a private company should be formed, with Joseph's two sons as directors. In July 1918, the Duke and his trustees conveyed the estate to the new company, subject to a mortgage of the balance of the purchase price still outstanding: £1.25 million (£77.5m). Thomas Beecham and his brother, Henry, had to sell enough of their father's estate to discharge this mortgage. By 1924 enough money had been raised and the Covent Garden property and the pill-making business at St Helens were united in one company, "Beecham Estates and Pills". The nominal capital was £1,850,000 (£170m) of which the Beecham brothers had a substantial share. The whole of the American side of the business was bequeathed to Henry.

Left: Thomas Beecham's factory built in 1877. Today it serves as the College Administrative Centre for St Helens.
Right: An advert for Beecham's Pills from 1909.

(ROBERT) MARK BEVAN

b. 1949

Mark Bevan

Mark Bevan is an author, historian, speaker, journalist and former editor of the Northwich Guardian. Over the last twenty five years he has written books and articles, given countless talks and established his own publishing business - Cheshire County Publishing (Chester). Mark has been an invaluable source of expertise for many would be authors who have "a tale to tell" but need guidance from a professional to bring their endeavours to fruition. It is safe to say that without Mark Bevan our village might never have had a coherent picture of its past.

Mark remembers the Guardian office in the 1970s when he was a reporter "bashing out the news" on a cast-iron typewriter "amidst a fog of cigarette smoke". He says the Guardian office became "the heart of the town centre... councillors, coppers, sporting contacts etc. would just wander upstairs for a natter... Gwili Lewis, the manager of the Memorial Hall, used to announce his arrival from the bottom of the stairs, with an incredible rendition of the Pathe News Cockerel".

Mark Bevan's own books are mainly local and regional works, including histories of Cuddington, Sandiway and Delamere Park. He is particularly interested in the two World Wars, with its devastating loss of young men, including four from his own family. Born and bred in the village, Mark can trace his maternal ancestors, in the area, back to the 17th century. He now lives in Hargrave, Chester, with his wife Olwen; they have two sons. Below are just a sample of Mark Bevan's fascinating books:

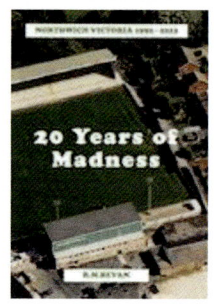

MRS J. W. PAULINE BOUMPHREY

1886 - 1959

Shire Champion - A bronze sculpture by Pauline Boumphrey.

Pauline Boumphrey was resident at Dalefords, Sandiway, from 1930 until 1937, although she always retained studios in London. She was an eminent American painter and sculptor, who particularly enjoyed working in oils and modelling animal bronzes. Pauline exhibited five times at The Manchester Academy of Fine Arts, seven times at The Royal Academy of Arts Summer Exhibition and at prestigious venues in Liverpool and Scotland. In Paris, she featured in the Salon des Artistes Français and was awarded an honourable mention in 1925.

Dalefords today, the home of Mrs Boumphrey in the 1930s.

Her main works are - a Design for a Memorial to the Women and Children killed in Enemy Action (1939 -1942); H. L. Cottrill Esq; Battleship: Grand National Winner; The Stallion: Robin Goodfellow; The Top of the Hill: Lady Nuttall; Down from the Mountains; Early days; An Old Favourite; The Young Stallion; From the Hills and Herontyre (both 1935); and Earl Haig, Grand National Winner and Windswept (all 1945).

Pauline was born Pauline Firth in Boston, Massachusetts, and after the death of her only brother, when she was four, was raised as a boy, developing a keen interest in horse riding and shooting. Once installed at Dalefords she often "rode to hounds" with the Tarporley Hunt gaining the respect of her fellow riders. She married twice, first in 1911 in London, to Richard Ford Haworth from Fallowfield, Lancashire, and then, in 1927, at Fylde Registry Office, to Joseph W. "Joe" Boumphrey, a British textile manufacturer. On one of her return visits to Boston, Pauline befriended Chief White Horse, of the Southern Yankton Sioux. She produced and presented him with a bronze bust of himself and, in return, he gave her his headdress, a bow case and pipe bag. The headdress, a fine Sioux war bonnet, sewn with 29 eagle feathers, bead and quillwork work in red, yellow, blue and white and suspending tassels of ermine, was sold at Christies, in 1995, for 4,000 dollars.

Chief White Horse of the Southern Yankton Sioux. It is not known if this is the war bonnet he gave to Mrs Boumphrey but it would have been similar.

Joseph Boumphrey died in Conwy in 1955 and Pauline returned to the USA to live on East 56th St, New York. She passed away whilst staying in Florida. A more detailed history of her life and work is held by the Smithsonian Institute in Washington DC.

In 1985, some years after her death, a book entitled *The Power of Animal Bronzes* by Pauline Boumphrey was published in America.

Three more animal bronzes by Mrs Boumphrey. Above - *Fighting Cock*; above right - *Earl Haig* and right - *Spaniel*.

***A Still Life with Summer Flowers in a Vase,* by Pauline Boumphrey. Oil on board, signed and dated 1953. 20ins x 24ins.**

MALCOLM COURTNEY BOYLE

1902 - 1976

Malcolm Courtney Boyle

Malcolm Courtney Boyle was a British organist and composer whose home, for 28 years, was The White House, School Lane, Sandiway. Malcolm was born in Windsor where he spent most of his childhood. His parents, Stephen and Agnes Boyle, had two other children: daughters, Mary and Elspeth. His father was the "Lay Clerk Tenor" at St George's Chapel in Windsor Castle and, as a boy, Malcolm served as a chorister at Eton College before becoming an organ pupil of Sir Walter Parrott at St George's. At 17 he was appointed organist and choirmaster of Holy Trinity Garrison Church and conducted the Windsor and Eton Orchestral Society. After taking his Bachelor of Music at Queens College, Oxford, Malcolm became Assistant Organist to Sir Walter Davies, again at St George's Chapel (1925-1932). He attended the Royal Academy of Music in London where he was granted an organ scholarship.

In 1932 Malcolm Boyle came to Cheshire as organist and master of the "Choristers of Chester Cathedral" but, as a divorcee, was dismissed by the Dean and Chapter when he re-married in 1948. His second wife, Ruby James, was still living at "The White House" in February 2015. In his capacity as an Examiner for the Associated Board of the Royal Schools of Music, a position he was appointed to in 1949, Malcolm travelled widely - to New Zealand, India, Hongkong and the West Indies. For Expo year, in Canada, he was chosen as one of a panel of specially co-opted musical adjudicators.

His most famous compositions are *Daughters of Zion* and *Thou, O God, art Praised in Zion*, which still enjoys a place in the musical repertoire of the Anglican Communion. For many years no published editions of either were available, only existing in manuscript form, the latter having been written down from memory by Dr George Guest, who had been a chorister at Chester Cathedral under Malcolm. Both were published well after Malcolm's death, by Paraclete Press. Fittingly, *Thou, O God...* was the introit at Dr Guest's memorial service.

From 1965, until just before his death, in 1976, Malcolm was organist at St John's Church, Sandiway. Malcolm Courtney Boyle is recorded in *The Book of Remembrance* in the Musicians' Chapel, London, and by a plaque in Chester Cathedral. In Sandiway, a brass plaque and two processional candlesticks were given to St John's Church in his memory.

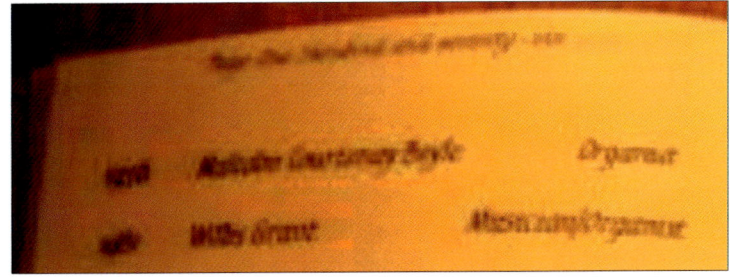

Left - Memorial to Malcolm Boyle in Chester Cathedral. Above - Malcolm's name in *The Book of Remembrance* in the Musicians' Chapel, The Church of St Sepulchre-without-Newgate, London.

JUDGE EDWIN COOPER BURGIS

1878 - 1966

Judge Edwin Cooper Burgis moved into The Small House, situated in the extensive grounds of Merlewood, Mill Lane, Cuddington, in the late 1930s and lived there until his death in 1966. Oxford educated, he was appointed the County Court Judge for Cheshire, Lancashire and Yorkshire, and was honoured with a Knighthood in June 1948.

Edwin Cooper Burgis in his County Court Judge's attire.
Photo: ©National Portrait Gallery, London.

At the start of the Second World War, Judge Burgis was made Chairman of the Lancashire and Cheshire Objectors Tribunal. It was he who made the final decision as to whether individuals could be excused from war service as conscientious objectors; he gained a reputation for his uncompromising attitude. This was born out on 6th April 1940 when Judge Edwin Burgis sustained a horrific knife attack. 24 year old clerk Henry Ballantyne Best's application for conscientious objector status had been dismissed by Judge Burgis and the following day, as the Judge was boarding the train on his homeward journey, Best stabbed him multiple times in his neck and back. The attacker ran off, but that night handed himself in, and was eventually sentenced to five years penal servitude for wounding with intent to murder. The surgeon who operated on Judge Burgis, at Ancoats Hospital, Manchester, said he was lucky to be alive but he still resumed his duties in June of the same year. Judge Edward Burgis was very philosophical about his ordeal, commenting that it was "...all in a day's work". Some years earlier he had shown his heroism, in WWI, when he was awarded several medals for bravery as a Captain in the Royal Garrison Artillery.

Judge Burgis was the son of Edwin and Isabelle Burgis and brother to Alice, Lucy, Sarah, Cecil and Dora. He married Edith May Stratton, from Littleover, Derbyshire and they had one daughter, Isabel Edith Burgis. On his death he left £106.086 (£1.8m).

Merlewood in the early 1900s. The lake in its grounds is known locally as "Thompson's Pool" after Merlewood's first owner, A. J. Thompson (page 87).

BOB CAROLGEES

b. 1948

Born Robert Johnson in Birmingham on 12th May 1948, Bob Carolgees is a comedy entertainer best known for appearing with a puppet named Spit the Dog. He lived at Kennel Cottage, Kennel Lane, Sandiway, before moving to Delamere Park. The name Carolgees came from friends, Carole and George Dunmore, who owned a record shop called Carolgees Records & Cassettes and a mobile disco, Carolgees Cabaret Disco. In the early 1970s, Carolgees ran a Disc Jockey and modelling school at 11A, Lord Street, Liverpool. After a five-week course, DJs and models were tested in front of an audience at the Sportsman's Club in the city centre.

Robert Johnson (Bob Carolgees) at the height of his fame, in 1982, with his puppet, Spit the Dog.
©alamy.com

Bob appeared on the Saturday morning television series *Tiswas* and later in its adult versions and *Saturday Stayback*. He first appeared in a guest spot on *Tiswas* on 31st March 1979, when the main presenter was Chris Tarrant. His first words to Bob after he'd seen his performance were, "You're going to be on the telly, it's great!" Clowning around with a monkey puppet called Charlie, Carolgees went down well with the viewing audience and after being invited back for several guest spots, he became a team presenter. Bob Carolgees, in pyjamas and headband, was also the *Tiswas* character Houdi Elbow, a comedy psychic and small-time magician.

Bob went on to work for eight years alongside Cilla Black in *Surprise, Surprise*; fronted pop/game show *Hold Tight!*, produced by Granada Television for Children's ITV; and a game show, *Concentration*. In the 1980s, at the height of his popularity, he featured in a series of Hellmann's Mayonnaise press and television commercials for eight years, dressed as an overgrown schoolboy. Bob Carolgees was the subject of *This is Your Life,* in 1994, when he was surprised by Michael Aspel at the Lyceum Theatre, Crewe. For over three decades Bob has entertained British armed forces around the world, including during the first Gulf War and the Balkan Conflicts. He was the first to entertain the troops during the Falklands War.

In 1991 Bob performed in the pantomime, *Jack and the Beanstalk,* at the Piccadilly Theatre, London with Cilla Black, Jean Boht and Patrick Mower. In 2013 he made a surprise return to show business, by agreeing to appear in the same production at Hull New Theatre and was quoted as saying, "What I had missed most was panto". He also temporarily came out of show business retirement to appear with all his old colleagues in *Tiswas Reunited* on ITV on the 16th June 2007. Recently he has appeared with Peter Kay in *Phoenix Nights*.

An early Spit the Dog puppet raised over £5,000 at a Christie's Auction in 2004. Bob has now separated from his wife and is living in Frodsham. Until recently he owned a candle shop there: Carolgees Candles. Bob's children, Natalie and Richard, still live on Delamere Park with their mother, Alison, who has since remarried.

ANDREW "ANDY" WILLIAM CARTER

b. 1949

Andy Carter is a retired track and field athlete who represented Great Britain in the men's 800 metres at the 1972 Olympics in Munich, West Germany. He finished sixth in a time of 1:46.55 but his recorded fastest time for the race is 1:45.12, in 1973, when he won the Amateur Athletic Association Championship at London's Crystal Palace. In all, Andy Carter improved the British record for 800 metres on three occasions and won the AAA title in 1970, 1972 and 1973. He held the British 800 metres record for many years, before Sebastian Coe broke it and went on to become double Olympic champion.

The logo for the 1972 Olympics in Munich.

Andy Carter as he is today, a coach at Vale Royal A. C.

The US magazine *Track & Field News'* annual world rankings placed Andy third at 800 metres in 1971, eighth in 1972 and sixth in 1973. At the European Championships in Helsinki, in 1971, he stood on the podium to receive a bronze medal, again in the 800 metres, with Yevgeniy Arzhanov (Soviet Union) and Dieter Fromm (East Germany) in a time of 1:46.16. In 1974 he won a silver medal, representing England in the Common Wealth Games in the 4×400 metre relay in Christ-church, New Zealand, in a time of 3.06: Kenya won the gold. Andy's other personal bests included - the 400 metres in 48 seconds, the 1,000 metres in 2:18.5 minutes (both in 1974) and the 1 mile in 3:59.3 minutes (1972).

Andy Carter was born on 29th January 1949, in Exeter, Devon, but now lives on Delamere Park, Cuddington, with his wife, Gill. They have three children and two grandchildren.

During his years of competing, Andy was a member of Stretford Athletic Club, Manchester, and is now a Middle Distance, United Kingdom Endurance Athletics Coach, working with a host of promising youngsters at Vale Royal Athletics Club which has produced 25 athletes who have represented their Country at Cross Country or Track and Field events.

DR PETER CHIVERS

b. 1922

Dr Peter Chivers holding the medals from his ten marathons.
Photo: Paul Wolfgang Webster.

In the heart of Cuddington, off Warrington Road, there is a driveway containing five detached dwellings. One of these, standing at the far end, is Heyridge and in its adjoining annex lives a wonderful gentleman: Dr Peter Chivers. Peter has run ten London Marathons and others in Berlin, New York and Paris. His latest was in 2000 at the age of 77. Through sponsorship for these events, Peter has made a great deal of money for charities, including the 69ers Youth Club, in Cuddington, a cause particularly important to him. Dr Chivers helped found this voluntary organisation and his generous donations have enabled the building to have major extensions. For this, and his efforts for the local community (Dr Chivers served 32 years as a Parish Councillor and was the last Chairman of Northwich Rural District Council), he was awarded the MBE in 1997.

Born in Cheshire, Peter was educated at Stockport Grammar School and studied medicine at Manchester University. After his first hospital appointment, as Casualty Officer at Preston Royal Infirmary in 1946, Peter joined the Merchant Navy and, two years later, the Royal Navy. In 1951, he started his career in industrial medicine, when he became the Works Medical Officer in Longbridge, Birmingham, with what was then known as the Austin Motor Company. Two years later he came back to Cheshire to join ICI, as the Medical Officer in their Alkali Division, where he worked until 1979. Before finally retiring in 1992, Peter was a part-time, self employed doctor for a number of companies and authorities.

Dr Peter Chivers has always been a keen advocate of keeping fit. He has cycled all his life and enjoyed running, tennis and squash. Although now suffering from macular disease, which means he can see very little, until recently, Peter was still out on his tandem every week. Proving his fitness three years ago, at the age of ninety, he cycled laps of Oulton Park, at the *Get On your Bike* event, when he was piloted round the track by his 76 year old brother, James. For many years Dr Chivers could be seen, regularly, out running with his youngest son, Steven. Even now, at 94, he tries to go out each Saturday morning and can be found on his running machine every day. Dr Chivers lost his wife, Jean, several years ago but has three surviving children, five grandchildren and two great grandchildren. In 2003 his entertaining book, *My Bizarre Naval National Service*, was published. The text was derived from the many long letters Peter sent back to his family whilst serving in both the Merchant and Royal Navy.

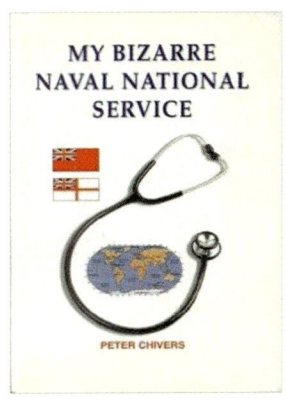

The front cover of Dr Chivers' book about his naval exploits.

PAMELA CLARKSON

b. 1946

Pamela Clarkson and her husband, Atta Kwami, who is also a prominent artist.

Pamela Clarkson is a professional painter and printmaker who moved into Poplar Farm, Cuddington in 1963 when she was seventeen. She has taught extensively in British art schools and travelled in North and South America, Europe, West Africa and the Far East. Pamela now divides her time between Ghana and Britain, with studios in Ayeduase, Kumasi, and Loughborough. She trained as a painter at the Manchester School of Art, followed by the Central School of Art and the Royal College of Art, London (1964-70) and studied printmaking at the University of Chile and the Catholic University of Santiago, Chile (1973-74). From 1975-78 she was a Research Assistant in Printmaking at the University of Wolverhampton.

The focus of Pamela Clarkson's work has moved from "expressive abstraction of a particular place, usually landscape" to "a more formal use of images of objects, found seen, glimpsed and remembered in and around life in Kumasi".

Pamela met her husband, Atta, in 1991 when she went to Ghana to set up a printmaking studio in the College of Art, Kwame Nkrumah University of Science and Technology. Pamela and Atta have since established a similar studio in their home in Kumasi which is now known as "Take Time Press". Pamela Clarkson is William Garner's (page 38) maternal Aunt.

Black Trees - one of a series of four painted between 1977-1983, when Pamela returned home to look after her mother. In the evenings she was free to walk along the lanes and Pamela writes, "In the night the sycamore trees, already high up on the ridges of the roadside banks, seemed to have doubled in size. The hollows of the trees, the branches, and the spaces within and around, stood out in contrast; thick complicated foliage flattened out into simple silhouetted shapes. With growing familiarity I attributed a sort of personality to each tree. ...They were worked and reworked many times until I got what I wanted which was a balance (more a tight-rope walk) between rage and tranquillity".

Just five of Pamela Clarkson's many impressive pictures. Below and then clockwise - *Blue Almond*, *Zigzag Pots*, *Two Pots Zigzag and Pinch* (from Pamela and Atta's exhibition entitled "Grace", dedicated to Atta's mother, 2012/13); *Combs Cambridge 11*, (from a suite of twelve linocut prints, 2013); and *Common Day,* an earlier landscape from 1981/2 (Touchstones Gallery, Rochdale).

THE CLOVER FAMILY

With their inherited wealth and social life set in some of the highest society in the realm, the Clover clan are typical of the many families who settled in mid-Cheshire in the nineteenth and early twentieth century. The head of the family, Charles Matthew Clover, was born in Birkenhead in 1877. His father had made the family's fortune as a shipbuilder and his son, Charles, was an "Average Adjuster", expert in the law of marine insurance, with offices in Liverpool and London under the name of Charles McArthur Clover and Stone. At first the "Clovers" lived at Dalefords (page 13) but, in the mid 1920s, Charles and his wife, Florence, built a new home in Kennel Lane, Sandiway, and named it Fox Hills.

Their eldest daughter, "Betty" - real name Marian Elizabeth Marconi Jessie Clover (1911-1997) - married four times: first, Geoffrey Charles Fontmay Adams, in St Mary's Church, Whitegate in 1935; second, Lionel Gascoyne-Cecil (1941); third, Baron William Gaspard Guy Romilly (1966), and fourth, Col. Edward John Sutton Ward (1986). Geoffrey Adam's father was a prosperous chemist who had homes in Australia and London. Lionel Gascoyne-Cecil, who died in 1962 leaving £126,000 (£2.5m), was the Great Grandson of the Marquis of Salisbury and Lady Mary Sackville-West. William Romilly's lineage can be traced directly to Sir John Romilly, statesman, created 1st Baron in 1863; his first wife was Diana Sackville West, daughter of 4th Baron Sackville of Knowle, Kent. He died in 1983, at the age of 84. Her final husband, Edward Ward, was the Grandson of the Earl of Dudley, of Dudley Castle, in the County of Stafford. Belonging to one of the West Midland's most prosperous families, he could also boast a strong pedigree and was Edward VII's godson. He died at the age of 93.

William G. G. Romilly

Florence Whiteford Bell Clover, the youngest of the Clover children, was the only one to be born in Wrexham where her parents lived before moving to Sandiway.

Marion Clover saw a great deal of the world during her life and always travelled in the lap of luxury. Whilst married to Lionel and living in Camberley, Surrey, the couple sailed to South Africa and Texas on the Cunard liner, Queen Elizabeth, and with William she journeyed to New York and Canada many times on vessels from the White Star Line. Marian Clover had outlived her fourth husband, by seven years, when she passed away, childless, in 1997.

Charles and Florence had three other children: Charles George Clover (1909-1996), Annette Helen Bell Clover (1913) and Florence Whiteford Bell Clover (1916). All but the last were born in Bidston, Birkenhead. Charles George Clover married an Argentinean, Monica Thorne Ricketts, and they had one child.

Charles Clover's wife, Florence Eliza Helen Clover (née Bell), the daughter of George Bell, a prominent Canadian Barrister and relative of Alexander Graham Bell (inventor of the Telephone), also had a colourful life. For 22 years she had an affair with Sir Edmund Fleming Bushby, a wealthy Liverpool cotton merchant and broker. When Sir Edmund died, in 1943, he left an estate, worth £43,000 (£1.8m) to his wife, Lady Elaine Bushby, but Florence claimed £12,084 (£.5m) as hers. She maintained that Sir Edmund Bushby had been holding it in trust for her. By 1921 Charles Clover had been living beyond his means and in 1931 was bankrupt. Sir Edmund advised Mrs Clover to give him any securities for safe keeping. Sir Edmund gave his mistress an allowance and expensive gifts including four Rolls Royce's, ponies and greyhounds, and it was thought that it was he who funded the £10,000 (£.5m) needed for the building of Fox Hills. As so often happens in these cases, the matter ended up in court where Florence was questioned in the witness box for five and a half hours. Wearing a brightly coloured, flowered silk scarf, over a black dress, and surrounded by mementoes from her romance, Mrs Clover read from diaries, accounts and bundles of love letters. She alleged that Marconi, the famous radio pioneer, who was a close friend (her daughter "Betty" was his godchild and named after him), had given her £5,000 (£280,000) which she took straight to Sir Edmund for safe keeping. Sir Edmund realised that, after his demise, the allowances he was giving to Florence would inevitably stop, so in 1936 he asked his lawyer to draw up a will, secretly leaving £30,000 (£1.9m), which was to be given to his mistress on his death, but in a second will, in 1939, no such provision was made, which made the first invalid.

This photograph of Florence Clover (1877-1965) was taken in the 1940s. She was born in Toronto, Canada.

Sir Edmund Bushby.
Photo: ©National Portrait Gallery, London.

The press, inevitably, made the most of the saga with headlines such as "Infatuated Knight poured out money" and "Love's Loans Lost". It was said that, at one time, Charles was going to "give him (Sir Edmund Bushby) a thrashing" but one of Sir Edmund's gardeners intervened. In 1948 the case was finally dismissed and Florence Clover, now sixty, is quoted as saying, "If I had to do it over, I would act the same way. After all, it kept my family together," and her husband, a sprightly seventy year old, to have replied, "You did your best for our children," before pouring the champagne he had saved for the occasion.

Fox Hills, built for Florence Clover, her husband Charles and their four daughters, and thought to have been paid for by Sir Edmund Fleming Busby, Florence's lover, at a cost of £40,000 (over £2m).

MAURICE DALE COLBOURNE

1894 - 1965

Maurice Colebourne as Brutus in *Julius Caesar*. He played Brutus twice in 1922 and 1925, in the Shakespeare Memorial Theatre, Stratford.

School registers and travel documents indicate that actor and writer, Maurice Dale Colbourne, was born at Gorstage Hall (page 5). It is possible that the Colbourne family were staying there when the confinement occurred as Annie Ashworth, the wife of the Hall's owner, Oliver Ashworth (page 103), and Maurice Colbourne's mother, were first cousins. As an actor, Maurice Colbourne was known for films such as The Magic Box (1951), Arms and the Man (1932) and I'm Alright Jack (1959). He worked alongside famous stars: Peter Sellers, David Attenborough, Terry Thomas, Ian Carmichael, William Hartnell, Denis Price and Robert Donat to name but a few. Maurice Colebourne was also a versatile Shakespearean actor and had an extensive career on the stage.

Whether the Colbourne family's sojourn in Gorstage was prolonged is uncertain but it is known that by 1901 they were settled in Beckenham, Kent. Maurice Colbourne's mother, Henrietta Leonora Krabbe, was Argentinean, and his father, Louis Colbourne, a surgeon. With five servants and their own governess, Maurice and his older siblings, Harold and Nora, had a comfortable childhood. Formal Education for Maurice began in 1912 at Repton School, Derbyshire, where he rubbed shoulders with Basil Rathbone, famed for his iconic screen portrayal of Sherlock Holmes. Colbourne was instrumental in starting the school's first Drama Association and when he went up to Oxford he was President of their Dramatic Society. Passenger lists at the time show that the Colbourne family travelled widely, to North and South America, Canada and New Zealand.

Left - Maurice Colbourne as Sir Hugo Cramp QC in *Brothers-in-Law* (1956) and right - as the bride's father in *The Magic Box* (1951).

Maurice Colbourne was a Governor of the Shakespeare Memorial Theatre and in 1928 he formed a partnership with fellow actor, Barry Jones (1898-1981), in order to tour Canada. They put on many Shakespearean productions there and were given the blessing of George Bernard Shaw in staging his own plays, "...so long as they are well done!" Maurice knew Shaw well, and in 1930 wrote a book entitled *The Real Bernard Shaw*. His other publications, include a play entitled *Charles the King,* but it is as an actor he will be remembered. His portrayal of the complex character, Brutus, in Julius Caesar, was said to be particularly moving. In his later years Maurice lived at 48, Camden Hill Square, London, but died, on September 22nd 1965, at Le Catiorot, St Saviours, Guernsey, leaving £55,881 (nearly £1m). Maurice Colebourne is not to be confused with the more recent actor, Roger Middleton, who adopted his predecessor's name.

STEVEN JAMES "STEVE" COPPELL

b. 1955

Steve Coppell is a former member of the England football team who played for Tranmere Rovers and Manchester United. He was a highly regarded right winger, known for his speed and work rate. He broke the record for the most consecutive appearances for an outfield Manchester United player – 207 from 1977 to 1981 – which still stands today. In a cup final against Notts. County, he scored the quickest recorded goal, at under eighteen level: twelve seconds. Born in Liverpool, on 9th July 1955, for most of his playing career Steve Coppell lived at Delamere Park, Cuddington.

Despite interest from top clubs he chose to join lower league Merseyside club, Tranmere Rovers, as he wanted to study for a degree in economic history at the University of Liverpool. In 1975, Manchester United made an offer for him of £60,000. Coppell signed and was still able to complete his degree whilst playing for them. In all he made 38 appearances for Tranmere and scored thirteen goals. For United there were 322 appearances and 53 goals.

Steve Coppell playing for England against Belgium on 12th June, 1980, in the UEFA European Championship Finals, Group B. The rest of the team were: Ray Clemence, Phil Neal, Kenny Sansom, Phil Thompson, Dave Watson, Trevor Brooking, Ray Wilkins, David Johnson, Kevin Keegan (captain), Tony Woodcock. The manager was Ron Greenwood; the venue the Stadio Comunale, Turin; the score 1-1 and the attendance: 15,186.
Photo: sporting-heroes.net

In 1977 Steven James Coppell received a call-up to the England team for the country's final qualifying game for the 1978 FIFA World Cup, against Italy, at Wembley. Coppell played and England won 2–0 but did not qualify for the finals. His England career concluded with 42 caps and seven goals. After suffering a knee injury, in the 1883 World Cup against Hungary, he struggled on for a little longer, but in October 1983, after three operations on his knee, the final one to no avail, he announced his retirement, aged just 28.

Since then Steve Coppell has managed Bristol City, Brighton & Hove Albion, Manchester City, Brentford and, most notably, Crystal Palace and Reading, both of which he took from the English second tier to each club's greatest-ever success in the Premier League. He is currently the head coach of the Kerala Blasters of the Indian Super League.

A Manchester United shirt from 1978 - 1979, typical of the ones Steve Coppell would have worn.

HENRY "HARRY" DEWHURST

1866 - 1931

The Oaklands, Gorstage. Harry Dewhurst lived here before moving to Dalefords.

In 1902, Harry Dewhurst moved into Dalefords, Sandiway, (page 108) having stayed for a year or so at The Oaklands in Gorstage. He was another of the village's cotton magnates who had made his fortune in the Lancashire textile industry. Born in St Asaph, Denbighshire, Harry grew up at Oughtrington Hall, Lymm, where his parents, George Bakewell Dewhurst and Frances (née Mann), were considered "Lord and Lady of the Manor". They and their offspring lived in fine style, with twelve "servants" and an estate extending to over one and a half thousand acres.

Harry's father, George Dewhurst, was one of two brothers who founded the firm G. and R. Dewhurst (of Sylko thread fame). The family owned cotton spinning mills in Manchester, Preston and Walton-le-Dale. George died in 1891 and Harry found himself having to take on far more of the running of the firm. Higher Walton Mill (in Walton-le-Dale) had 77,2888 spindles and 1,168 looms, and Cuerden Mill (Preston) 67,432 spindles and 1,032 looms: two of the largest mills in Lancashire. Well over 800 operatives were in full time employment from 1870 onwards and the firm won high accolades at exhibitions in Vienna, Philadelphia and Paris.

Robert Cyril Dewhurst

Once retired Harry Dewhurst put his energies into politics and charity work. He was the Unionist MP for Northwich (1918-1922) and gave generously to many good causes. On 17th November 1910, he invited the children of Sandiway School to a firework display at Dalefords and afterwards each child received a bun, an apple and a firework. Following WWI Harry Dewhurst restarted the annual Sandiway and District Horticultural Society Show, at his home, which attracted people from miles around. Harry Dewhurst married Ethel Maud Norris, in 1890, and they had one son, Robert Cyril Dewhurst, who wed Rhoda Wilbraham, the daughter of Hugh Wilbraham of Delamere House (page 93). Harry and his brother, Cyril Dewhurst, were two of the principal founders of Delamere Forest Golf Club and Harry its first chairman (1910-12). At his death, Harry Dewhurst was worth £16,415 (nearly £1m). Harry's elder brother, George, died in action in 1916 and his widow Annie Maud married the multi millionaire, Walter Jones, who occupied Blakemere Hall (page 50).

Oughtrington Hall, Lymm, the home of the Dewhurst family.

ARTHUR DODD

1919 - 2011

Arthur Dodd served in the British Army during WW2 and was a Prisoner of War at Auschwitz III (Monowitz), a sub-camp of the notorious Auschwitz. His home was in Blake Lane, Sandiway. After leaving school, at 15, Arthur became an apprentice engineer in Northwich before moving to the Weaver Navigation Company in 1937. In September 1938, he nearly lost his left foot when it became trapped between a ramp and a turning wheel and needed extensive physiotherapy for his injuries. He was not considered fit enough to join up but his HGV license enabled him to enlist as a military driving instructor for the Royal Army Service Corps.

Arthur Dodd pictured on the front of *Spectator in Hell*, which tells his moving story.

At the beginning of WW2 Arthur Dodd served as a volunteer in France and was involved in the Dunkirk evacuation. Later, he was posted to North Africa and saw action at Tobruk. After Tobruk, Arthur and an injured colleague were captured by the enemy at Badir, in the Western Desert, and held in a number of ordinary, Italian, Prisoner of War camps before being transferred to Auschwitz III (Monowitz) in 1943, a labour camp only five miles away from the better-known extermination camp of Auschwitz II (Birkenau). Monowitz was under the direction of the industrial company I.G. Farben who were building a synthetic rubber and liquid fuel plant there. They housed over 10,000 Jewish slave labourers, PoWs and forced labour from all over occupied Europe.

Colin Rushton, the author of *Spectator in Hell* and himself a Sandiway man, knew Arthur well. Colin and his wife, Pat, travelled back to Auschwitz, with Arthur, when the BBC were filming Arthur's story.

When Arthur and the Prisoners of War disembarked they noticed dozens of bundles of clothing that had just been left by the rail tracks, and as they were marched to the concentration camp and factory where they would be working, he tells of a teenage, Jewish girl, stripped to the waist who was being savagely whipped by an SS officer. Arthur Dodd and the other PoWs attempted to get between him and the bleeding girl but the officer pulled out his pistol and threatened to shoot Arthur, who was at the front. A Wehrmacht soldier warned him that he meant what he said so the British troops stepped aside and the officer resumed his whipping.

The filth of Camp E715, with its accompanying smell of burning flesh from the crematorium at nearby Birkenau, was to be Dodd's home for the next 14 months. During his imprisonment he witnessed the mistreatment and killing of Jewish inmates at the camp by their SS guards, including Jews hanging from the gallows in Auschwitz, and several pushed off high scaffolding. In late 1944, the British heard a noise outside their huts. On going outside to investigate, they saw about a thousand Jews, old men, women and children, walking towards Auschwitz II (Birkenau) on the other side of the perimeter wire. The children were playing and singing as they passed. Once they had gone, the men returned to their huts in silence. They had been told in the past of the fate of such columns of walking Jews. Arthur's life was frequently in danger too. During an air raid on 24th August 1944, Dodd and other PoWs were in a shelter which was hit by a bomb, killing 38 British prisoners and wounding several, including Dodd.

On 23rd January 1945, four days before Auschwitz was liberated by the Red Army, in the coldest winter Poland had experienced for years, the British PoWs were given the option by their German guards to either start walking eastwards towards the Russians or westwards towards the Americans. Arthur Dodd chose the latter. In the weeks of walking, when the temperature often dropped to minus 25 degrees, men froze, and some starved to death. As they walked, they passed the partially snow-covered bodies of hundreds of dead Jews, some of whom had died from cold or their exertions, while others had been shot. Those prisoners who had greatcoats, shared them, and they slept huddled together to stave off the cold. In the towns they passed, they witnessed the slaughter by the retreating Nazis. On reaching Regensburg, in Germany, Dodd and his colleagues were finally liberated.

The War over, Arthur Dodd returned to working for British Waterways, Northwich, and after battling Alzheimer's disease, he died peacefully on the 17th January 2011, aged 91. A campaign had been launched to raise the £500 a week needed to cover the cost of his full-time care. He left a wife, Olwen, two children, six grandchildren and ten great grandchildren. Arthur Dodd's full story is told in the book, *Spectator in Hell,* by Colin Rushton and in the television documentaries, *Satan at His Best* (1995), and the BBC's *Auschwitz: The Forgotten Witness* (1997). In the latter programme Arthur Dodd returns to Auschwitz to find the location of Camp E715, and tries, unsuccessfully, to gain admission to the I G Farben plant to claim the 14 months back wages he says they owed him for his forced wartime labour there.

Auschwitz III (Monowitz)

JOHN DOUGLAS

1830 - 1911

John Douglas

John Douglas's birthplace and family home was Park Cottage (now Littlefold), Sandiway. He was one of the most highly regarded architects of his time who left a lasting imprint on Cheshire which few could equal. Wonderful examples of his work are to be found throughout North Wales and the North West. Substantial, elaborate chimney stacks (often with "barley sugar" twists), romantic Germanic turrets, oriel windows and occasional Dutch gables, are all Douglas trademarks. In mid-Cheshire, they can be spotted in villages such as Arley, Great Budworth, Hartford and Whitegate; on the Duke of Westminster's estate, and in the towns of Winsford and Northwich. In the city of Chester, there are many fine examples, including the east side of the lower part of St Werburgh St, Grosvenor Park Road, and the icon of the city, the Eastgate Clock, which was erected in 1899 to celebrate Queen Victoria's Diamond Jubilee two years before, in 1897.

Pictured are: top - Littlefold, said to date from the 17th century; below - a blue plaque, positioned in 2003, to commemorate the place of Douglas's birth.

Despite never having lived in Sandiway during his professional life, Douglas retained an affection for the place of his birth. He continued to own land in the village which he referred to as, "My little estate at Sandiway". His greatest legacy to the locality is St John's Church. He donated the land on which it stands, drew up its design plans, and was a major contributor to building and furnishing costs, donating the East Widow and £1,000 (over £100,000) for the cost of the chancel. The lych gate was also designed by Douglas and both it, and the church, were designated listed buildings in 1986. He was responsible for other dwellings in the parish: Abbotsford (Warrington Road); Forest Hey and Sandiway Manor (Norley Road); Magpie Cottage and Model Cottage (Chester Road), and The Homestead (now Redwalls) and Croft House (Weaverham Road). In the Church of St Mary, Weaverham, there is a window given by John Douglas in memory of his parents and sister.

An early photograph of St John's Church, Sandiway. The foundation stone was laid by the Earl of Mansfield in 1902 and the building completed in 1903, apart from the tower with its embattled parapet which was added about ten years later. The difference in the stone work indicates its original height.

ANTHONY "TONY" DOW

b. 1948

Tony Dow

Tony Dow is best known as the director of BBC television's *Only Fools and Horses,* starring David Jason as "Del" and Nicholas Lyndhurst as "Rodney". The programme was voted Britain's Best Sitcom in 2004. He has also directed the TV series *UFO.* (1993), *Bob Martin* (2000) with Michael Barrymore; and *Birds of a feather* (1989). Tony lived on Ash Road, Sandiway, from about 1963 until 1970.

Tony Dow started his career as assistant stage manager with Eastbourne's Devonshire Park Theatre in 1966 and, after six months, went on to study stage management at RADA. There followed some twelve "happy" years working in theatres all over the country, including the West End, America and South East Asia doing musicals and plays. So when Tony joined the BBC he was already an experienced director. His first day in 'Light Entertainment' was with the children's television programme, *Blue Peter,* where he was worried about his lack of experience with a camera but he was reassured that cameramen were aplenty and it was his skill with actors that was needed. After a week of studio management he joined the *Only Fools and Horses* team which he always thoroughly enjoyed. Tony writes of his surprise when Ray Butt, the then director of *Only Fools and Horses*, left to become Head of Production at Central TV and John Sullivan, the script writer, and David Jason both went to "the powers that be" and asked for Tony as Ray's replacement. Tony went on to direct 24 episodes, more than any of the other series' six directors. He worked with the *'Only Fools...'* team from 1988 until 2002 and rejoined them in 2014 for a Sports Relief Special, aired on March 14th, with guest star David Beckham (the famous footballer) and entitled *Beckham in Peckham*. In all, as a director, Tony Dow has 84 credits to his name including - as well as those already mentioned - *Ain't Misbehavin'* (1994); *Roger, Roger* (1999-2003); *Blind Men* (1997); *Bergerac* (1991); Green Green Grass 2005-2009; Lee Evan's *So What Now* (2001) and *Stella* (2014-2016).

Tony Dow is the oldest of four sons born to Alan and Rosamund Dow when they lived in Walnut Lane, Hartford, near Northwich. Alan worked for ICI and it was after he and Rosamund (a teacher) divorced that Tony came to live in Sandiway with his mother and three brothers: Simon, Adam and Oliver. He was educated at boarding school in Caterham, Surrey, where his Grandfather had been Headmaster during the war. Tony now lives in London with his wife Su-Lin and the couple have two children, Moli (23 years) and Arthur (22). John Sullivan, the writer of *Only Fools...* was best man at Tony's wedding and his brother, Simon, became chief executive of the Guinness Trust and received a CBE in the 2015 honours list.

WILLIAM DRONSFIELD

1846 - 1939

William Dronsfield lived at Sandiway Lodge (page 5) for 35 years. When his father, James Dronsfield, died in 1881, William and his brother, Joseph, inherited the Atlas works in Oldham, Lancashire. The business, established in 1860 by James himself, acquired fame as the largest manufacturer of card grinding and card making machinery, for the cotton industry, in the world. In 1891 it had a capital of £50,000 (£4.5m) in £50 (£4,500) shares and William Dronsfield and his co-directors were looking to expand alongside carrying on business as colliery proprietors and quarry owners. William had become a partner in 1867 and held the position of an active chairman up to the time of his death. He received the CBE, in 1920, for his services to municipal affairs in Oldham and was elected an honorary life member of the Institute of Mechanical Engineers. His son, James, followed suit in 1912.

The blue plaque on the Dronsfield Works office building.

William Dronsfield
Photo: Mark Bevan Collection

William Dronsfield was one of those who decided to escape the murk of Industrial Lancashire and in 1905 he brought his second wife, Sarah Ellen Brown, to live at Sandiway Lodge. His first wife, Selina Smethurst, the mother of his three grown up children: James, Joseph and Agnus, had died in 1896. William was also to lose Sarah, in 1918, but lived on for a further 21 years, at "The Lodge", and came to be known as the "Grand Old Man" of Sandiway. On his 90th birthday, in 1936, he treated his staff and their partners, 37 in total, to dinner and a visit to the theatre in Chester. William Dronsfield is buried in Chadderton Cemetery, Oldham, and his effects amounted to £84,274 (nearly £2.5m).

A painting of "Messrs Dronsfield Bros, Oldham", in 1908.

In 1909 William's daughter, Agnes, married the **REV'D R. J. B. PATERSON-MORGAN** (1879-1966). He was curate at St John's Sandiway (1908-1910) and then Rector of Bangor-on-Dee until 1920; finally returning to Sandiway Lodge to live out his retirement. Known locally as "PM", he took a keen interest in politics and education, but his special legacy is the detailed records, written on cards in his own hand, of the war experiences of 74 servicemen who returned from the Great War to his Bangor parish. He interviewed every single man; to have such details is very rare. There is a stave in St John's Church donated by "PM" in 1935.

ROBERT "ROB" AND JAMES EASTAWAY

ROB EASTAWAY is an author and speaker whose main aim is to popularise mathematics. He is best known for his books, including *Why Do Buses Come in Threes?* and *Maths for Mums and Dads,* which were both best sellers. His first book, *What is a Googly?*, an explanation of cricket for Americans and other newcomers to the game, was presented as a gift, by Prime Minister John Major, to President George Bush at Camp David in 1992. Some of Rob's books have appeared in several languages. He is a keen cricketer and was one of the originators of the International Rankings of Cricketers. Rob is a former puzzle-writer for *New Scientist* magazine, President of the UK Mathematical Association for 2007/2008 and has appeared frequently on BBC Radio 2, 3, 4 and 5 Live. Rob Eastaway is also the Director of Maths Inspiration, a national programme of interactive shows, that have reached over 100,000 teenagers in the last ten years and which involves some of the UK's leading maths speakers. He gives talks that range from small interactive workshops to keynote lectures in front of an audience of several hundred. A former pupil of The King's School, Chester, Rob has a degree in Engineering and Management Science from Christ's College, Cambridge, and is a lifelong follower of Lancashire CC spending his summer weekends playing the game.

JAMES EASTAWAY is a renowned baroque oboist. It was at The Kings School, Chester, that he first took up the modern oboe at the age of eleven, but only considered a career in music after teaching himself to play the baroque oboe whilst studying medicine at Edinburgh University. Following a successful audition for the European Community Baroque Orchestra in 1991, he has divided his working life between music and medicine, working part time as an Accident and Emergency doctor. James has performed all over the world with the major British period instrument orchestras and groups such as Orchestra Champs Elysees, Amsterdam Baroque and the Australian Chamber Orchestra. He works most regularly with the English Baroque Soloists, Orchestra Revolutionnaire et Romantique, Orchestra of the Age of Enlightenment and the London Handel Orchestra. He has taken part in over fifty recordings and played principal oboe for many prominent conductors including Sir Charles Mackerras, Sir John Eliot Gardiner and Sir Roger Norrington. During 2000, as part of the 250th anniversary of Bach's death, James was a regular player in Sir John Eliot Gardiner's Bach Cantata Pilgrimage and, as part of BBC Radio 3's *Bach Christmas* in 2005, James was invited to play the Bach concerto for oboe d'amore. In 2003 he took part in the first complete performance of Berlioz epic *Les Troyens*, in Paris. He has taught regularly at the Royal College of Music, Royal Academy and Trinity College of Music and for the Academies Musicales de Saintes.

Robert and James are the sons of Jack and Joyce Eastaway (both now deceased) of Bridge Close, Cuddington. They have two siblings: Andrew, and Anne, a consultant microbiologist.

SIR JOHN ELPHINSTON

1924 - 2015

Sir John Elphinston

Sir John Elphinston lived at Pilgrims, Churchfields, Sandiway, until his death in 2015. He was a nephew of Sir Alexander Logie Elphinston, 10th Baronet, and succeeded his Uncle to the full title of "11th Baronet Elphinston, of Logie, co Aberdeen and Nova Scotia" on 16th December 1970. His ancestry can be traced directly back to William the Conqueror and his wife, Matilda of Flanders.

Sir John was the son of George Thomas Elphinston and Gladys Mary Congdon. He was educated at Repton School, Derbyshire, and in 1942 gained the rank of Lieutenant in the service of the Royal Marines. In 1950 he graduated from Emmanuel College, Cambridge, with a Bachelor of Arts degree and then trained as a chartered surveyor, becoming a Professional Associate, Royal Institution of Chartered Surveyors (ARICS). Between 1956 and 1983 he was a land agent with ICI and from 1983 until 1988 a consultant with Gandy & Son, Land Agents and Chartered Surveyors, Northwich.

John and Margaret Elphinston

On 23rd May 1953 he married Margaret Doreen Tasker and they had four children who were all brought up in Sandiway: Alexander Elphinston (born 1955) who is now the 12th Baronet; Charles (1958); Andrew (1961) and William (1963). The heir apparent to the baronetcy is the current baronet's eldest son, Daniel John Elphinston (born 1989). Lady Elphinston still lives locally.

Below is a delightful family photograph of John and Margaret Elphinstone with their four sons who were all brought up in Sandiway. Left to right - Alexander, William, Charles and Andrew.

ANNIE LOUISA FALCON

1834 - 1899

Soon after her marriage to Charles Falcon, an attorney-at-law in Liverpool, on 4th February 1863, Annie Louisa Falcon (née Green) and her husband moved into Forest Hey, Sandiway (page 90). The strong links between the Green family and that of Elizabeth Gaskell, the famous English writer, make Annie Falcon worthy of note. The two families' prolific correspondence, including some 1,000 letters, are held by The John Rylands University Library in Manchester, under the title "The Jamison Archive". Several are written by Annie from Forest Hey. Since their days together at Glasgow University, Annie Falcon's father, the Reverend Henry Green (1801–73), minister of Brook Street Unitarian Chapel, Knutsford, had been a trusted friend and colleague of William Gaskell, Elizabeth Gaskell's husband. Charles Falcon's first wife, Bessie Gaskell, was William's sister and Annie's mother, Mary, was an intimate confident and correspondent of Elizabeth, who described Mary as a friend, "to open my mind to". Both couples had four daughters of similar ages, who were, in turn, very close.

Annie Louisa Falcon

Annie was born at Heathfield, Knutsford, the third of seven children: Emily, John, Annie and her twin brother (who was still born), Mary, Alice (who died when she was four) and Isabella. Annie went to stay with the Gaskells when she was a child and, as she practised the piano, Mrs Gaskell would be writing her novels in the corner of the room. In her letters, Annie comments on how kind Mrs Gaskell was to let her do this. One Christmas the Gaskells went to stay with the Greens and Mr Gaskell read to them all from Charles Dickens' newly published book: *A Christmas Carol*. The two families' social circle included the Brontes, John Ruskin and Charles Dickens. At his home, Henry Green ran a successful boarding school for the sons of gentlemen which included Clement Wedgewood, the great grandson of Josiah Wedgewood, the internationally renowned potter.

Above are William and Elizabeth Gaskell. Mrs Gaskell was an English novelist and short story writer during the Victorian era. Her novels offer a detailed portrait of the lives of many strata of society, including the very poor, and are of interest to social historians as well as lovers of literature.

Annie and Charles had four children, all born at Forest Hey. The first, Maxwell, died at 17 months after being scalded in a bath of boiling water. His nurse had slipped away to fetch some cold and the toddler stepped into the tub. Annie was expecting her second child at the time and (Mary) Emma was born later in the year (1865). Another girl, Isabella, followed and finally, Charles Gordon Falcon, in 1869.

Annie was to be left a widow, with three children to bring up, when 64 year old Charles died unexpectedly, in February 1875. He left £25,000 (over £2m). At the time the couple were living at The Largs, Hesketh, Southport, but by the September Annie had sold her home for £2,000 (£162,000) and her new address became Lisbon Cottage, Weybridge, Surrey. Another tragedy was to hit Annie when her only brother, John Green, a Judge of the High Court in Bombay, was killed in an avalanche on 28th July 1883, on the island of Ischia, in the Bay of Naples. Annie died on 31st May 1899 at 38, Wynnstay Gardens, Kensington.

Henry Green, Annie Falcon's father and Minister of Brook Street Chapel, Knutsford, 1827–1872.
Henry has an honoured place in the town for his book entitled *Knutsford: Its traditions and History with reminiscences, anecdotes and notices of the neighbourhood* (1857). He was a Latin scholar and had published an edited facsimile of *Whitney's Emblems* and also a book on Euclid. For a time he ran a night school and frequently gave talks and lectures. At his successful boarding school, *Heathfield*, the 17 pupils listed in 1851 came from Liverpool, Bolton and Manchester and included Clement Wedgwood from Etruria in the Potteries.

John Philip Green, a high court judge in Bombay and the only surviving brother of Annie Falcon. He died in an earthquake on the island of Ischia, in 1875, leaving a wife and three sons.

DAVID FLORY

b. 1959

David Flory is an excellent example of a "local boy made good". He was born on the eleventh of the eleventh, 1959, to Beryl (née Marsh) and George Flory, on Fir Lane, Sandiway. Until his recent retirement, David was the Chief Executive of the National Health Service Trust Development Authority and before that the Department of Health's Director General of NHS Finance, Performance and Operations. It was whilst working for the latter that David Flory gained his CBE.

David Flory CBE, truly a "local boy made good".

After attending Cuddington County Primary School and Sir John Deanes Grammar School, Northwich, he completed a degree at the University of Hull. When he joined the Department of Health, in 2007, David already had over twenty years board level experience in National Health Service bodies in the North East of England, including being the first Chief Executive of NHS North East.

In December 2013 he was said by the *Health Service Journal* to be the fourth most powerful person in the English National Health Service with the third highest salary. When David left his post, in March 2015, Jeremy Hunt, Secretary of State for Health said (in a press release):

"I have immensely valued David's wise counsel, advice and judgement, and in particular his ability to find solutions to problems that often appear intractable. But most of all I have come to admire the values that lie underneath that ability: a real commitment to doing the right thing for patients and safer, more compassionate care."

Throughout his career David worked tirelessly for the National Health Service. Aware of the financial problems it faced he was consistently frank and to the point in his many presentations and speeches. He steadfastly stressed the importance of sustainability and having strong relationships between all parties in the system. In 2013 David spoke about the financial pressures on the Service but how it was important not to lose sight of its core purpose, namely to provide high quality care for patients. In December 2013 he warned that there were at least thirty NHS hospital trusts facing serious problems and that the National Health Service would have to "take out capacity" or cut services. David Flory has one sibling,

David Flory receives his CBE from Princess Anne in 2009.

Michael Flory, who works for the United Nations in Vienna. David is married to Judith and they have three grown up children: twin girls - Kate and Lucy - and a son, Matthew.

DEREK GALLOWAY

b. 1944

On a bandstand, at St Anne's-on-Sea, Derek Galloway attempts to hold a melting ice cream and play the trombone at the same time. A now famous photo taken by his wife, Trish.

Derek Galloway is a musician who has been the vocalist for the Temperance Seven jazz band since August 1978. *You're Driving me Crazy* and *Pasadena* were two of the bands earliest hits. Elsie and Ted Galloway, with their two sons, Derek and his older brother, Ted, moved from Liverpool to Ash Road, Sandiway, on 17th March 1951, just before Derek's seventh birthday. This was to be Derek Galloway's home until he was 22. One of his amusing claims to fame is that he was the first pupil to enter Cuddington County Primary School when it opened in 1953. To be sure of the honour, and always keen to try something different from an early age, he jumped over the school fence before the gates opened.

Initially Derek's career was that of an engineer but in 1967 he started playing professionally with Dwight Gidney's Black Eagles New Orleans Band and then, in 1971, after two years with Ged Hone's outfit, teamed up with the Vintage Syncopators Jazz/Comedy band. Even though he joined the Temperance Seven in 1978, Derek continued to play trombone with a variety of New Orleans and parade bands, including The Red Rose, and the late Dennis Browne's Creole Serenaders. For the last seven years he has helped to run the Milneburg Boys based in mid-Cheshire, and in cooperation with Dave Copperwaite, presented visiting New Orleans musicians in Manchester. They have included Barry Martyn, Chris Burke, Les Muscutt and Chris Tyle. His performances have taken him all over Europe and Derek has played at events when Princess Anne and Lady Diana were the guests of honour, the latter several times. Derek lives with his wife, Trish, in Sale. They have three sons: Michael, Jonathan and Tony.

Derek Galloway, in the white jacket, with the Temperance Seven in 2015. They specialize in 1920s style jazz music.

WILLIAM GARNER

b. 1979

"William Wilde"
Photo: Muriel Watkin

"William Wilde" (real name William Garner) is a Manchester based dress designer and costumier. Such modern day super stars as Kylie Minogue, Lady Gaga, Rhiannon, Lily Allen, Miley Cyrus, Rita Ora, Paloma Faith and Paris Hilton have all worn his creations. William's sculptural, latex designs have been especially sought after, but he does experiment with other fabrics such as silk and lace. William makes all his own costumes and his hand stitching is exquisite. He has also been called upon to design the decor for nightclubs in London such as *The Box,* Soho, and in Los Angeles on "The Strip".

William Garner was born in 1979 at Hazeldene, a Victorian cottage on Warrington Road, Cuddington. As the house became too small for the family, his parents, Jennifer and Lyulph, and their other three children, Rachael, Jonathan and Imogen, moved four doors down the road to the home and butcher shop premises of William's grandparents, Bill and Eleanor Garner. In turn, Bill and Eleanor transferred to Hazeldene to enjoy their retirement years.

William has had a lifelong obsession with costume and clothing. As a child and teenager his family, teachers and friends recall that his every spare moment was spent absorbed in copying beautiful dresses painted by the great artists, although he now finds music and performance equally inspiring. William Garner studied at the University of Westminster and his first collection, entitled "The Butcher's Wife", was inspired by his mother and, indeed, his clothes still often have the distinctive stripes of a butcher's apron. William's aim is to be as iconic as Christian Dior. We must wait and see.

Four examples from William's extensive collection are shown here. Visit the website - williamwilde.com - to see the full range and celebrities wearing them.

EDWARD GRAHAM-WOOD

1918 - 2001

An Ocean Iron Works advert from 1905.

Edward Graham-Wood bought Delamere Manor (page 8) from George Wilbraham in 1953, and dwelt there until 1967. Edward's grandfather, Edward Wood, founded the Ocean Iron Works, Salford, in 1878. The firm were constructional engineers who won large contracts all over the country and overseas. Some of their more interesting buildings in Manchester are Ship Canal House, the Allied Newspapers offices, Lewis's store in Market Street and Telephone House in Salford. In 1935 they supplied the steelwork for the new extension to Manchester Town Hall: approximately 5,000 tons. They had other offices at 88, Cannon Street, London EC. They were renowned for their excellent organisation; the Company's massive steel structures were erected with amazing speed and accuracy.

Above is Sir Edward Graham-Wood, Mr Edward Graham-Wood's father.
Photo: ©National Portrait Gallery, London.

A member of the Cheshire Forest Hunt and Cheshire Polo Club, Edward Graham-Wood kept stables full of hunters and polo ponies, and was related to Sir Kingsley Wood, the wartime Chancellor of the Exchequer. Edward's father, Sir Edward Graham-Wood, died in 1930, leaving £79,548 (£4.5m) to his family. When his mother, Dame Dorothy, followed suit in 1956, she left £39,623 (nearly £1m) to be divided between her two sons, Edward and David. It can only be imagined what wealth Edward Graham-Wood had amassed by the time of his death in 2001. There is no public record.

Aerial view of the Ocean Iron Works in 1949.

An advert for the Ocean Iron Works from 1940.

THE HAWKE FAMILY

JULIAN STANHOPE THEODORE HAWKE (1904-1992) bought The Old Mill House (formerly Brooklands), Mill Lane, Cuddington, in the 1930s. He was a direct descendent of Admiral Sir Edward Hawke, perhaps the greatest sailor of the eighteenth century. Other noteworthy ancestors were the Admiral's son, Bladen, the 2nd Baron Hawke, who was MP for Saltash for six years and Martin, the 7th Baron, an accomplished cricketer who captained Yorkshire for 28 years, England on four occasions, and was always on the winning side.

The Hon. Julian Stanhope Theodore Hawke, resident at The Old Mill House for about sixty years.

Admiral Sir Edward Hawke

Theo, as he was known, was born in India and educated at Eton and King's College, Cambridge. After university, he returned to India to work for a trading company before coming back to England, in the early 1930s, to take up an appointment with Glazebrook Steel and Co., a cotton trading company in Manchester, where he remained until his retirement. Theo was an Honorary Commissioner for Taxes, and during World War II, a Squadron Leader in the RAF, training troops in West Africa and then overseeing barrage balloons in the Crewe area.

Julian Stanhope Theodore Hawke, 10th Baron Hawke of Towton, with The Old Mill House, his home in Cuddington, in the background.

In 1933, Baron Hawke married Griselda Bury. They had two daughters, Sarah (born 1935) and Catherine (1940), but the marriage was dissolved in 1946. In 1947 Georgette Davidson became Theo's second wife. Their children were Nichola (1949), Edward (1950), Vanessa (1957) and Julia (1960). Julia died in a diving accident off the Galapagos Islands in 1997.

Like his father, **EDWARD GEORGE HAWKE** (1950-2009) was educated at Eton College and had a distinguished military career. From 1970 to 1973 he served in the First Battalion Coldstream Guards before rising to the rank of Major in the service of the Queen's Own Yeomanry between 1973 and 1993. He was appointed Honorary Colonel of The Cheshire Yeomanry and awarded the Territorial Decoration (TD). As a Fellow of The Royal Institute of Chartered Surveyors (FRICS), he became a qualified Chartered Surveyor in Manchester. On the death of his father in 1992, Edward succeeded to the title Baron Hawke of Towton, as the 11th Lord Hawke. He continued to

7th Baron Martin Hawke

live at the Old Mill House and, in 1993, married Bronwen James. Their children, William and Alice, were born in 1995 and 1999 respectively. Edward died in 2009, making William the 12th Baron Hawke at the age of 14.

WILLIAM MARTIN THEODORE HAWKE was educated at Stowe School and is currently at The Royal Agricultural College, Cirencester.

A charming holiday snap of the Hawke family. Left to right - Edward, William, Bronwen and Alice.

The Baron Hawke coat of arms.

The Old Mill House (then Brooklands) Mill Lane, Cuddington. This photograph was taken some years before the Hawke family moved in.

Edward Julian 8th Baron Hawke and father of Theo. His elder son, Bladen Wilmer Hawke 9th Baron Hawke (1901-1985), was an active Conservative peer in the House of Lords and a Church Commissioner. He married Ina Faure-Walker and they had seven daughters: Caroline, Annabel, Cecilia, Lavinia, Rowena, Prunella and Olivia. Theo became the 10th Baron Hawke on the death of his brother in 1985.

Frances Alice Wilmer, the wife of Edward Julian Hawke and the mother of Bladen, Theo and Veronica.

Theo's six children. From the top and clockwise - Edward, Julia, Sarah, Vanessa, Catherine and Nichola.

LORD CHRISTOPHER HINTON OF BANKSIDE

1901 - 1983

Lord Christopher Hinton was one of the 20th century's most eminent engineers. He made an enormous contribution both to energy generation technology and later to politics as an active member of the House of Lords. Widely recognised as the father of the civil nuclear industry in the UK, he brought enthusiasm and energy to everything he did. *The Dictionary of National Biography* describes Hinton as, " one of Britain's relatively few truly great engineers." He lived for ten years of his life at Browne Knowle, Chester Road, Sandiway, near the Round Tower.

Lord Hinton of Bankside.
Photo: ©National Portrait Gallery, London

The son of a stern, primary school headmaster, Christopher Hinton was born in Tisbury, Wiltshire, and educated at Chippenham County Secondary School. In 1926, after serving an engineering apprenticeship with the Great Western Railway in Swindon, and only two years study, he graduated with a first in Mechanical Sciences from Trinity College Cambridge. On leaving Swindon, the GWR's engine erector said to him, "I'm sorry you're going, you are the best apprentice craftsman I've ever had working for me." In the same year Christopher Hinton came to Northwich to work as a research engineer for Brunner Mond and Co. Ltd., soon to be part of ICI. This included responsibility for the ordering, installing, upkeep and repair of instruments on all Works in the Brunner Mond group, with a permanent staff of eight men. Just a few months later he was given responsibility for equipping a new £129,000 laboratory and he was still only 26 years old. By the incredibly early age of 29, Christopher Hinton became the chief engineer of ICI's Alkali Division. At Brunner Mond it is said that Christopher Hinton transformed a fossilised department into one with great status and authority. This was a sign of things to come, as his engineering departments thereafter were, without exception, extremely efficient with systems of programming and cost control far ahead of their time.

Christopher Hinton, the driving force behind civil nuclear power in Britain.

During WW2 Christopher Hinton worked as deputy Director-General for the Ministry of Supply, directing the construction of explosives filling factories. For Christopher, it was always much more important to be successful than clever and, with this in mind, he changed the chaos which threatened an ammunition shortage, similar to that in WWI, into a system that met changing weapon demands smoothly and swiftly.

The most heroic part of Christopher Hinton's life began in 1946, after the war, when he was charged with producing, with the utmost urgency, the fissile material the Government required for atomic bombs. He was appointed to the UK Atomic Energy Authority to head the design and construction of the UK's nuclear facilities, including Harwell, Windscale (now Sellafield), Springfields, Capenhurst, Calder Hall and Dounreay. All were opened on time and within budget and his attention to detail was unerring. Qualified engineers were scarce and he found that continuous teaching was crucial. Christopher Hinton was a stern taskmaster; he could be kind but also scathing, and never interested in popularity. Calder Hall, opened in 1956, contained the first plutonium-based nuclear reactors in the world to feed electrical power into a national grid. It was over these years that Christopher was associated with other leading scientists such as Sir John Cockcroft, Sir William Penny and Sir Leonard Owen (page 57). The sensitivity of Christopher Hinton's work at this time meant security around his home, in Sandiway, had to be tight and a private detective was installed in a newly built annex in his garden.

During Sir Christopher's time at the Central Electricity Generating Board he commissioned the Hinton Cup, a piece of silverware that would be presented annually to the power station that displayed good housekeeping in the workplace. The citation to go with the cup reads, *"This cup is presented to the Power Station judged to have reached the highest attainment in economy and efficiency of operation and maintenance with particular reference to attractiveness and good housekeeping."*

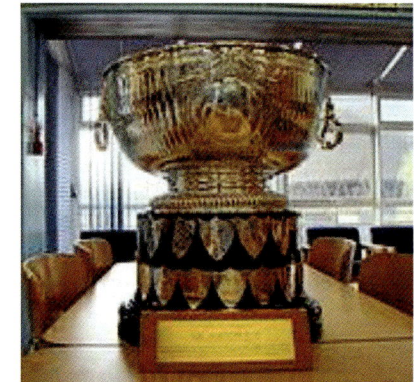

The Hinton Cup

In 1951, after refusing the honour on three occasions, he was knighted for services to industry. His family and friends had argued that he would offend the Queen if the knighthood was not accepted and this he did not want to do. In 1953, Sir Christopher and his wife were invited to the Queen's Coronation. The family recount how the couple were surprised by a royal corgi under their dining table! 1958 saw Sir Christopher appointed as the first chairman of the new Central Electricity Generating Board, established to supply electricity in bulk to the retailing area boards. It was at this point that the family moved to London. In 1965, Sir Christopher Hinton received a life peerage. He chose. for his title, the name of Bankside Power Station in London, an oil-fired station operational from 1891 until 1981 and now Tate Britain.

This newspaper cutting, from 1951, shows Sir Christopher outside Buckingham Palace with his wife, Lillian, and daughter, Susan, after receiving the KBE.

In semi-retirement Lord Hinton was a very successful first Chancellor of the University of Bath; a special advisor to the World Bank; Chairman of the International Executive Committee of the World Energy Conference (1962-68); and President of the Council of Engineering Institutions (1976-1981). In this last role he was involved in the final stages of creating The Fellowship of Engineering, now the Royal Academy of Engineering, and introducing an annual Distinction Lecture (1977), which was renamed the Hinton Lecture when he retired as President. It is still the Academy's premier yearly event. He was made a Fellow of the Royal Society, and in 1976 awarded the Order of Merit, a distinction restricted to only 24 members and considered the most exclusive club in the world.

It was while he was working in Northwich that Christopher Hinton met his wife, Lillian Boyer, a local Winnington girl, and they came to live in Sandiway. She had been employed as a "tracer" at Winnington Works. Christopher Hinton's employers were not happy about their relationship but true love prevailed and Christopher did not lose his position! Older residents remember the couple frequently enjoying a drink in the Blue Cap Hotel, a short walk from their home on Chester Road. He was 6' 6", a tall, lean, impressive figure and his wife, somewhat shorter, at 5' 2". They had one child, Susan Mary (1932-2014), who married Arthur Charles Mole, son of Sir Charles Mole, director-general of the Ministry of Works.

Christopher Hinton's wife, Lilian Boyer, in her younger days.

The family's memory in Sandiway is kept alive by the Lillian Memorial Fund, set up by Lord Hinton in 1974, the year following his wife's death. It was to provide " the additional provision of comfort... for the residents at Sandiway Manor Care Home" which is situated on Norley Road, not two minutes from the Hinton's former abode (page 48). Now named "The Hinton Trust", the original fund of £10,000 (£100.000), today covers the cost of all the home's bed linen and towels; Christmas presents and weekly entertainment for the residents; and three special lunches, in March, August and December, for everyone involved at "The Manor". "The Lady Hinton Reflective Garden" is to be found in the grounds for the residents' enjoyment. Lady Hinton served on the Committee at the Home for ten years, from 1947 at its foundation, until she and her husband moved to the capital in 1957. Although her death occurred in London, Lady Hinton is buried near her childhood home in Witton Cemetery, Northwich. Lord Hinton lived at Tiverton Lodge, Dulwich Common, from about 1965 until his death.

On 26th October 1983, there was a Service of Thanksgiving for the Life and Work of Lord Christopher Hinton at Westminster Abbey. The same day, at the Institute of Mechanical Engineers, a bronze bust was unveiled of him which joined busts of George Stephenson, James Watt and other great engineers of the past. It was also ensured that Lord Hinton's name would be remembered for years to come on 10th July 2010, at Magnox Limited's annual open day, when Locomotive number 37409 was named "Lord Hinton". Direct Rail Services (DRS) provide Magnox Limited with specialist rail transport services, essential for transferring spent nuclear fuel from its reactors to Sellafield, Cumbria, for reprocessing. DRS. gave Magnox the opportunity to name one of its

Richard Mole with his grandfather's name on Locomotive 37409. Photo: Richard Fleckney.

newly refurbished locomotives, by running a competition for employees to suggest an appropriate name for the engine. Lord Hinton's grandson, Richard Mole, was at the Direct Rail Services depot, in Crewe, to unveil his grandfather's nameplate. His name is also perpetuated by a ship, *MV Lord Hinton*, a coal-carrier ordered by the Central Electricity Generating Board in 1984 shortly after his death.

Lord Hinton was not only interested in Science; he was knowledgeable about history, architecture and literature. An avid reader of Jane Austen, he knew every house in Bath connected with her novels. In his memorial address at Westminster Abbey it was said that even at 25 "...after only nine years' work and education, Christopher Hinton had emerged with a formidable combination of skills, creativity and intellectual power - with the perfect blend of practical and theoretical training which the engineering profession today finds so elusive". Some of his final words to students at Bath enshrined his optimism for the future:

"You are going out into a changing world... but all change is a challenge. I am not offering you any pity. What I wish is that I was young enough to share the challenge with you."

Another newspaper cutting showing, from the left - Sir Christopher Hinton, the Queen, Prince Philip and James Ashley, at the opening of Trawsfynydd nuclear power station, in 1963.

WILLIAM HORNER

1827 - 1897

William Horner, about 1890.
Photo: Mark Bevan Collection

William Horner established a factory in Cuddington which was by far the largest ever seen in the locality. In 1874, he bought The Bryn, a detached eighteenth century house on Bag Lane, and in its outbuildings he manufactured cream cheese and clotted cream. By the early 1880s, William Horner's Creamery was sending vast quantities of dairy produce all over the North West and the Second World War saw the transformation of the site into a modern unit, processing millions of gallons of milk a year and, at its peak, employing between 250 and 300 men and women. In 1963 Horner's was bought by Express Dairies who joined forces with Eden Vale two years later. The old Creamery was converted to accommodate the production of yoghurt with fruit added. "Ski" yogurt, as it was called, was a best seller and was sent throughout the UK. Over 50,000 tonnes of "Ski" was produced at the Cuddington site and more factories were established as far afield as Australia. Nestle purchased the business in 2002 for £145 million but by 2007 all output stopped and production moved to Europe.

William Horner was born at Fingerfield House, Grewelthorpe, in the North Yorkshire Dales, to Mary and George Horner. At just 19 he left home to seek his fortune. Initially William was a "barrow boy" selling fruit in the centre of Liverpool. It was at this time that he married Ann Coops from Knutsford. They had eleven children but Ann died of peritonitis in 1871, only three weeks after giving birth to twin girls.

Workers inside Horner's Creamery a century ago.

Soon after Ann's death, William brought his family and business, now that of a "cheese factor", to Smith's Lane, Weaverham. His enterprise flourished, soon outgrowing the new premises, so when William heard that The Bryn was empty, he was keen to relocate once more, particularly as the Cheshire Lines Railway had just arrived in Cuddington. The new station would mean faster access to the important markets of the North West and beyond.

Horner's bottles. Left to right - Little Jack Horner Orange Juice, two pint milk bottles and a third of a pint cream bottle.

William Horner set to work with energy and expertise. He harnessed the power from one of the mill wheels below The Bryn to drive a hydraulic ram pump which sent water along a pipe up the fields to his creamery, and as the most economically efficient way of using the waste from a creamery was to feed it to pigs, he built extensive piggeries adjacent to his factory. Once manufacture was underway, William maximised efficiency by creating a shuttle system of several horse and cart teams, travelling to and from the station, taking butter, cheese and cream and returning with empty churns and coal for the furnaces. Horner's Devonshire Clotted Cream was particularly famous and in 1884 William Horner patented an apparatus for *"Separating the Cream from the Milk"*. His method made the cream particularly rich and creamy. He set up Tom, his eldest child, as manager of a Creamery in Prees, Whitchurch, and in the 1890s started building four workers cottages in nearby "Pinfold Hollows" which his third son, George Horner, completed after William's death.

Horner's clotted cream was sold in indigo and crimson print bottles.

In the summer of 1877, William married 25 year old Elizabeth (Eliza) Helen Mountford, from Staffordshire They had two daughters: Beatrice Charlotte and Rosa May, who died when she was seven. The family are buried in St Mary's Churchyard, Weaverham, including William's first wife, Anne. *William Horner and his Creamery*, a book by Jill E. King, gives a full account of the man, his family and the Creamery until it's final demolition in 2011 to make way for the Eden Grange housing estate.

Above - The Horner family's final resting place in St Mary's Churchyard, Weaverham. To the right: Top - The Bryn, William Horner's home on Bag Lane, (demolished in 1985). Middle - one of the first lorries bought by George Horner in the 1920s. Bottom - With Horner's iconic chimney towering above them, the creamery workers, with their horse and cart teams, gather outside for a photograph.

WALTER JOHN HENRY JONES

1866 - 1932

From about 1896 until 1923, Walter Jones's home was Blakemere Hall, Sandiway. A fine sportsman, he was part of the winning polo team at the 1908 Olympics, even though, at 42, he was the oldest competitor in the Great Britain squad. *The Polo Encyclopaedia* states, "The standard of polo elegance in the 1890s is exemplified by Walter Jones, number one in the Rugby team, the side that had such an enormous influence on polo in Britain." He played primarily for Rugby, but also his own Blakemere side which he formed on his arrival in Cheshire.

Great Britain's Gold Medal winning Polo team at the 1908 Olympics, held in London. Walter Jones is second from the left.

Walter John Henry Jones was born at The Elms, Daresbury, the son of William and Lucretia Jones, and educated at Harrow and Jesus College, Cambridge. His father was the owner of Jones Brothers Cotton Mills, Tyldesley, Leigh, and extremely wealthy. Walter inherited the factory and much of his father's fortune. It was a five story building with large rectangular windows, a water tower with a dome and a tall circular chimney. The engine house stood to the north and a reservoir to the east. In 1891, Jones Brother's and Co., or Bedford New Mill, as it was known, had 53,000 spindles and 970 looms. In 1918, the mill was bought by Courtaulds.

George Littleton Dewhurst

On 31st January 1910, Walter married Annie Maud Dewhurst, the widow of George Littleton Dewhurst (another Lancashire cotton magnate) of Beechwood, Lymm and Aberuchill Castle, Scotland. Walter's step children, Margaret and Lieutenant George Littleton Dewhurst, lived with their mother at Blakemere, but George, who served with the Rifle Brigade, was killed in action on the Somme on 1st July 1916, aged 24.

The Blue and *The Red Rigi* by J.M.W. Turner.

Walter Jones was a collector of first edition books and important watercolour paintings. He was particularly fond of the artist J.M.W. Turner's work and purchased his *The Blue Rigi, Lake of Lucerne, Sunrise* and *The Red Rigi*, along with other valuable Turner drawings such as *Venice, the Mouth of the Grand Canal, Barnard Castle, Peterborough Cathedral and Ludlow Castle*. The collection passed to Jones' widow in 1933, and was sold after her death at Christie's on 3rd July 1942. In 2006, *The Blue Rigi* sold again for £5.8 million which was a record for the auction house. The *Red Rigi* has been in Australia since 1947, and hangs in The National Gallery of Victoria, Melbourne.

Hurlingham Lodge today.

Walter Jones's other pastimes were fishing, big game hunting and raucous parties. Mark Bevan, in his wonderful book, *Cuddington and Sandiway 2000,* paints a picture of him as a rather eccentric millionaire. At Blakemere he is said to have spent £4,000 (over £425.000) on new stabling for his many polo ponies, but immediately decided they wouldn't do and ordered its prompt replacement. Today the stables are the core of the Blakemere Craft Centre. From a first floor room, the gentlemen would "wager on cock-fighting (though illegal) in the courtyard below". Apparently these were boisterous occasions attended, it is alleged, by the Prince of Wales (Edward VII) who travelled incognito, as "Mr Peters". After these events, local joiners were employed to repair the furniture. Walter Jones also commissioned a full-sized model of a deer, set on wheels, which was frequently pulled out into the grounds by his butler, so that his master could take pot-shots at it from his sitting room window.

He spent thousands on the grounds, with a glorious display of azaleas and rhododendron bushes and in the nearby fields could be spotted his herd of highland cattle. In June 1902 Sandiway School's log book records that the 135 or so pupils each received a medal, "the gift of Mr Jones of Blakemere" to celebrate "the *expected* (it had to be postponed as the future king was ill) coronation" of Edward VII. The hall itself contained both a smoke and billiard room and a bathing pool. 13 staff were employed, including a butler, a footman and various female domestics and "grounds men". Blakemere was demolished in 1950.

Walter John Henry Jones spent the latter part of his life (1924-1932) at Hurlingham Lodge, Fulham, near the scene of his Olympic victory. On his death, on April 14th 1932, he left a net estate of £327,406 (£21m).

Blakemere Craft Centre today. The old Hall has long gone but the shops around the courtyard are thought to be the original stables where Walter Jones kept the "best string of polo horses in Great Britain".

CHRIS KELLY

b. 1940

The White Barn, Chris Kelly's birthplace and childhood home.

Born on the 24th April 1940, Christopher Kelly was brought up at the White Barn, Cuddington, where his parents, Jim and Madge Kelly, were licensees for over thirty years. Chris has produced, written and presented numerous radio and television programmes covering current affairs, drama, the cinema, the arts, food and drink and travel. Educated at Downside School, a Catholic independent school in Somerset, followed by Clare College, Cambridge, he started his career, in 1963, with Anglia Television as a continuity announcer, and then moved to Granada TV, in Manchester, before turning freelance.

Chris Kelly
Photo: Mark Bevan Collection

Chris Kelly wrote and produced 500 editions of the family film programme, *Clapperboard*; was principal commentator on *World in Action*; travelled the world with *Wish You Were Here* and presented *Food and Drink* for many years. He also worked extensively for regionally based television companies, including Anglia, where he wrote and presented an arts programme, *Folio*, and Tyne Tees, where he co-presented the first regular ninety-minute live programme on British television: *Friday Live*. Chris Kelly produced series one and two of *Soldier Soldier* for Central, the first of which won the Gold Award for Best Drama Series at the 1992 Houston International Film Festival. His career, as a TV producer, has also included *A Line in the Sand*, *Monsignor Renard*, *Without Motive* and five series of *Kavanagh QC*.

Chris has written several books: *The Telebook, Kellyvision* which won a silver medal at the New York Festival of Film and Television, *The War of Covent Garden, Taking Leave, A Suit of Lights* and *Forest of the Night* which is loosely set in and around Cuddington.

Six of Chris Kelly's publications. *Forest of the Night* is an adventure tale about the mysterious and dangerous events that confront a young boy on his return to the village where he was born. It is loosely set around Cuddington.

DIGBY LAWSON

1880 - 1959

Sandiway Manor today, the home of Digby Lawson.

Sir Digby Lawson, 2nd Baronet, was a director, and later chairman, of Fairbairn, Lawson, Combe, Barbour Ltd. The business was based in Leeds and Belfast and was, at the time, the largest maker of textile machinery in the world. During the 1930s, Digby Lawson also became a director of the highly powerful and influential ICI Alkali Division, Winnington, and this is when he made his home at Sandiway Manor, Norley Road.

The dashing Captain Digby Lawson.
©Imperial War Museums (HU 118678)

Born in Leeds, Sir Digby Lawson was educated at Winchester College, Hampshire, and Trinity Hall, Cambridge, where he obtained a BA. In WWI he was a Captain in the service of the 19th Hussars and a Major in the Yorkshire Yeomanry where he was mentioned in despatches. On 1st June 1915 Digby Lawson was awarded the title of Baronet, and between 1919 and 1926 was the JP for Somerset, and President of the summary courts in Cologne. However, he is particularly noted for his personal life. It was his first bride, the 19 year old beauty, Iris Mary Fitzgerald, who caused him problems. After their marriage, in 1909, Iris, very speedily, bore him three children: Daphne, John and Patrick, but in 1914, with the outbreak of war, Digby left home to serve with his regiment on the Rhine and Iris appears to have felt neglected. His suspicions were aroused when her letters began to cool and she did not bother to visit him when he returned for a spell of hospital convalescence. He decided to have Iris followed and she was seen going into the Grosvenor Hotel accompanied by a man but, when confronted, Lady Lawson refused to say who the gentleman was. Only her signature could be found on the hotel's registration forms and, in 1919, Sir Digby Lawson was granted a decree nisi against Lady Iris Mary Lawson because of her misconduct with an unknown male. The anonymity of the gentleman fuelled speculation amongst society and the newspapers loved the story. To add to his misery, Arthur, his younger brother, had fallen in action in 1918. His second wife, Victoria Frances Maud Baille, died in 1931 at the age of 31, and Ruth Mary Gimson, his third spouse, in 1961. Sir Digby had three children: James and Arthur from his second marriage and Simon from his third. All his sons had distinguished careers but James was accidentally killed whilst serving with the Fleet Air Arm aboard *HMS Glory*, in the Pacific, on June 18th 1946.

James Lawson, son of Digby and Victoria, was killed whilst flying in 1946.

Quite why Sir Digby Lawson took up a directorship of ICI's Alkali Division is uncertain but there is a connection between Sir Digby and the Brunner family, of Brunner Mond Ltd., a prominent forerunner of ICI. William Worsley and his wife Joyce (née Brunner) were close neighbours of the Lawson's in Yorkshire and Joyce was the granddaughter of Sir John Brunner, the founder of Brunner Mond. The Worsley's daughter, Katharine, is the present Duchess of Kent and Sir Digby Lawson was her Godfather when she was christened in 1933. Sir Digby also had connections with the Devonshires of Chatsworth House, Derbyshire, and the Percys of Alnwick Castle, Northumberland, who had the same ancient ancestry as the Lawson family. The Duchess of Devonshire regularly sent gifts to Sir Digby's children

No doubt the charm and relative privacy of Sandiway appealed to Sir Digby Lawson after his rather eventful life but he always retained his connection with his father's vast company, Fairbairn Lawson Combe Barbour Ltd., and was their chairman from 1946 until his death. At the time of his death, in London, Sir Digby Lawson had amassed £50,000 (£1.25m).

Left - Victoria Frances Maud Baille Digby Lawson's second wife and mother of James and Arthur Lawson.
Photo: ©Andrew Paterson/SHPA

Right - Ruth Mary Gimson, third wife of Digby Lawson, and mother of Dr Simon Digby Lawson; she outlived her husband by two years.
Photo: ©alamy.com

Col. Sir John Charles Arthur Digby Lawson (on the left), son of Digby Lawson and his first wife, Iris Fitzgerald. This charismatic man was considered by many to be the best Squadron Leader in the 8th Army.

THOMAS CECIL LOCKER

1891 - 1964

Thomas Cecil Locker

Thomas Cecil Locker lived at Beechfield (more recently Lamb's Grange), off Forest Road. He was managing director of the firm Locker Group Ltd., Warrington, which was established by his grandfather, also Thomas Locker, in 1878. Thomas Locker, Sr was the first person in the world to weave wire on a steam powered loom, a method of manufacture which had a revolutionary effect throughout the trade. He was succeeded by his two sons, James and Thomas, and it was the former, who was the father of Thomas Cecil Locker. The business were contractors to the British Admiralty War Office, the Indian Office and all principal railway companies. They were also Crown Agents for the Colonies and their clients included Wembley Stadium and Korean Oil Rigs.

By 1914 Thomas Cecil Locker was appointed "Engineer in Charge responsible for the running of the works". The highlight of his career was the design and manufacture of two special types of heavy wire weaving looms, with "improved let-off motions and a radical alteration of shuttle carrier and necessary gear".

Thomas C. Locker's grandfather, Thomas Locker.

Thomas Cecil Locker's father, James T. Locker, was Mayor of Warrington.

Thomas Cecil Locker studied engineering in Manchester, where he gained a first class honours degree and, later, lectured at Warrington Technology Institute on all aspects of engineering. His son is the actor and film director James Challis Thomas Locker, known for *The Spanish Farm* (1968), *The Big Spender* (1965) and *The Spirit of Crazy Horse* (1990). Thomas Cecil Locker left £111,346 (over £2m). After his death, his wife continued to live at Beechfield well into the 1970s.

Beechfield, the home of Thomas Cecil Locker and his family.

(SUSANNA) MAUD MAINWARING

1843 - 1930

Park Cottage (now Littlefold), the home of Maud Mainwaring for forty years.

Maud Mainwaring is one of those ladies whose determination and strength of character still shine through, even though it is 86 years since her demise. Maybe it has something to do with the fact that both her parent's families can be traced back to the time of William the Conqueror and that, through her father, Maud is listed in the "Blood Royal of Britain". She was a prominent member of the RSPCA and an active and generous benefactor to the villages of Over Peover, her native parish, and Sandiway, where she spent the last forty years of her life.

Animals in the early 1800s were mainly seen by the British public as commodities for food, transport and sport and the RSPCA lobbied parliament throughout the nineteenth century to change this attitude. Due to their efforts, cock fighting and bear baiting were forbidden and standards were improved for "pit ponies" and in slaughter houses. In 1876, the Cruelty to Animals Act was passed, to control animal experimentation, and in 1911 Parliament passed the Animal Protection Act. During the First World War the Society's aim was to reduce animal suffering and provide swift and humane treatment for those hurt in the war. 2.5 million were admitted to the Army Vetinary Corps for treatment: horses, mules, dogs, camels, bullocks, carrier pigeons and others were treated and over 85% returned for duty. When the war was over the NSPCA set up the Soldiers Dogs Fund to meet the cost of quarantining, until demobilised men could take their animals home. 500 kennels were specially built at Hackbridge, Surrey. A fund for sick horses raised over £250,000 (£12m) and, by the end of the war, the Fund became international. Miss Maud Mainwaring would have been actively involved in many of these issues and challenged any cruelty she saw. A newspaper article dating from her later years tells of an incident where she observed a horse being "ill used" and ordered her groom, William Porte, to follow the driver and stop him. She was said to keep wild black and white rabbits in the field next to her home.

Peover Hall, Maud Mainwaring's home until she moved to Sandiway in her 40s.

Maud Mainwaring was the seventh of nine children born to Sir Harry Mainwaring and his wife, Emma (née Tatton), at Over Peover Hall, near Knutsford. Her parents were considered to be "The Lord and Lady of the Manor of Peover". One brother, George, had died at 17 days old, the year before Maud was born, and she was to lose two more male siblings, Randle and Stapleton, at relatively young ages. Soon after her father's death, in 1875, Maud, her eldest sister Emma, and their mother, moved out of the Hall to allow her oldest surviving brother and the heir to the family estate, Sir Philip Tatton Mainwaring, and his family, to move in. Maud and Emma went to Park Cottage in Sandiway and their mother to Hartford Beech, Northwich, where she died in 1886.

Over Peover village benefited considerably from Maud's sojourn in their midst. In 1865, Sir Harry was instrumental in establishing an Educational Trust to provide for an improved school in the village and his daughter took a keen interest in the children's lessons and welfare, becoming a school governor when her father died. She introduced school holidays, regularly distributed prizes, listened to their singing, watched the drilling in the playground and gave tuition in sewing and diction. When living in Sandiway, Maud continued to take an interest in the school and in 1910 the "Mainwaring" family offered a plot of land and £425 (£45,000) for a new school and school house. On leaving the parish, Maud was presented with candlesticks by members of the church choir in testimony of their respect and esteem.

At the turn of the twentieth century, Maud Mainwaring became involved in the building of St John's Church, Sandiway. Apart from the money she raised for the pews and grounds, Maud collected, from the ladies connected to the Tarporley Hunt, for the cost of the West Window in memory of the late Captain Park Yates, from Sandiway Lodge (page 5), and when the tower was added to the church, in 1910, it housed a seven hundredweight bell provided by Maud. Throughout her life Maud Mainwaring continued to vigorously stand up for what she believed to be right and her charity work carried on undaunted. In 1903 she accompanied Lady Delamere from Vale Royal Estate, Whitegate, to the Chester Assizes over a dispute concerning a "permissive" path from Sandiway to Whitegate across Sandiway Golf Club, and newspapers of the time tell of generous legacies, often as much as £500 (approximately £50,000) to charities close to her heart. A bountiful lady indeed!

A horse float presented to the Army Veterinary Corps by the RSPCA in about 1915.

LADY HELENA MARY MOLYNEUX, THE COUNTESS OF SEFTON

1875 - 1947

A family photo, showing the Countess, taken at Croxteth during WWI.

Osbert Cecil Molyneux, 6th Earl of Sefton.

Lady Helena Mary Molyneux (known to her family as "Nellie") is to be particularly noted for her unstinting, selfless charity work and the detailed diaries which she kept from a few days before her marriage on the 8th January, 1898, until the day before her death, nearly fifty years later. The books are housed in the Liverpool Record Office and consist of 111 volumes contained in nine diaries and albums. Only 1918 is missing.

In the early years of her marriage, Lady Helena lived at Dale Ford, now Dalefords, in Sandiway (page 108). She was the third daughter of George Cecil Orlando Bridgeman, the 4th Earl of Bradford. On 8th January 1898 she married Osbert Cecil Molyneux, second son of William, the 4th Earl of Sefton. In 1901, Osbert Molyneux's invalid older brother, Charles, the 5th Earl of Sefton, died and Osbert succeeded as the Earl of Sefton number six. The couple left Dale Ford to take up residence at the family seat, Croxteth Hall, Liverpool. There are two entries in the diary that mention leaving Sandiway, "*...went over to Dale Fords... to settle about the removal of the furniture...*" (6th June 1902), and "*I went to Dale Ford for the day for the last time, it being now sold to Mr. Dewhurst...*" (July 1902). Her two sons, Hugh William Osbert Molyneux (1898) and Cecil Richard Molyneux (1899) were born at Dale Ford but her daughter, Lady Evelyn (1902), at Croxteth.

During WWI Croxteth Hall was used as a hospital for wounded soldiers and officers. On the 9th June Lady Helena notes, "*Our first batch of soldier patients came into the hospital - 12 from Alder Hey*". All the equipment needed was financed by Lord and Lady Sefton and over 1,000 officers were treated there until it closed in July 1919. Lady Molyneux's diaries show how involved she was in the welfare of the patients. She frequently accompanied them on outings in the local area, attended first aid classes and prepared flowers for her own and other hospitals, including Mill Road, Highfield and Heswall. She also volunteered at VAD headquarters which was a voluntary unit providing field nursing services, worked in hospitals in Belgium and London and at the Women's War Service Bureau, prominent in Liverpool at the time. Meanwhile, Lady Helena's husband was stationed in Cupar, Fife, so much of the management of "Croxteth" fell on her shoulders. The couple frequently travelled between Liverpool and Scotland to see each other. On 26th July, Lady Helena records, "*At one heard from Sir J. Barr that 11 officers were being sent us from Fazakerley at 4. Busy afternoon. At 5 few arrived rather unexpectedly for a bed. Florrie telegraphed that Laddo was starting with a draft for Salonika tomorrow - so I took the midnight train (after seeing the patients comfortably settled in)...*" It is assumed that "*Laddo*" is Lady Helena's husband.

The first injured men arrived at Croxteth Hall just nine days after Lady Helena learnt of the death of her youngest son, Cecil at the Battle of Jutland. He was just 16 years old. An entry on 31st May reads, "*The Battle in the North Sea began at 3.30 today & beloved Cecil was killed by a shell in his gun turret on the Lion, Admiral Beatty's flagship. We knew nothing until 3rd...*" and on 1st June Lady Helena records, "*Cecil was buried at sea at 6pm with 101 others from the Lion nearer the Norwegian than the Scottish coast, the service read by Capt Chatfield, the Chaplain being killed*", and on 12th June, "*Mother came at 5. The Memorial Service for Cecil and all who fell in the naval battle in West Derby Church at 6*". Lady Sefton lost her only daughter, Evelyn, on 26th June of the following year, at the age of 14.

Despite her, undoubted, strong desire to help those less fortunate than herself, the Countess was a lady of her time and shared the Molyneux family's interest in sporting activities. She was " one of the principal lady supporters of the sport of Coursing " and in 1921 was the "first woman to win the Waterloo Cup " with her dog "Shortcoming". A newspaper cutting in her diary headed "A Lady Lion Hunter" refers to the Countess of Sefton as "the adventurous Society Sportswoman who... recently shot her first lion in Abyssinia". Thankfully, no more are mentioned. She was a keen traveller and sightseer but most of her travelling was done with Osbert and, according to a cutting from the *Evening Express*, 28th August, 1947, "'Always a supporter of good causes she intensified this work after the death of her husband". Lord Sefton was 59 when he died and was succeeded to the earldom by his eldest and only surviving son, Hugh. In 1943, Lady Sefton left Croxteth Hall to live at Bridge House, Mossley Hill Drive, but visited regularly, spending much time in the gardens where she died on 27th August 1947.

Obituary notices for the Countess make many references to her work for charity. They refer to her " lifetime of public work" and as an "assiduous worker for many good causes in Liverpool". Her voluntary work included, the Liverpool Cathedral Building Fund, the British Legion, the St John's Ambulance Brigade, the Gordon Smith Institute for Seamen, where she was a dinner time waitress during WW2, and a number of boy's clubs. She made many generous bequests and shortly before her death bought a house in Falkner Square, Liverpool, "with a view to converting it into a hostel for aged women." The Countess of Sefton left £78,851 (£3m), an enormous sum for a woman in those days, and Osbert, a mind blowing £1,758,376 (over £100m).

Croxteth Hall

THOMAS MOORE

1873 - 1938

White Lodge has changed very little since the time of Thomas Moore.

Thomas Moore lived with his wife, Mary (née Crane), at White Lodge, Norley Road, in the early part of the 1900s. He and George H. Brock, who joined him as co-director in 1906, owned the Northwich Carrying Co. Ltd., Cotton Works Yard, Baron's Quay, Northwich. The Company was formed in 1883 by Thomas's father, a local slate merchant (also named Thomas Moore) to transport salt and chemicals, between Northwich and Liverpool for Brunner Mond, when it was established in 1874. Eventually, river transport became less economically viable, due to the challenge from road and rail and the business wound up in 1932. The Northwich Carrying Co.'s name was sold for £5 and they became Moore and Brock.

The firm's considerable premises, in Northwich, were used to house their Builders' Merchant's business. By the 1950s, they had other offices in Chester, Crewe, Leek and Warrington. Its large, four-storey warehouse was burnt down in the 1980s, some say in suspicious circumstances. By the 1990s, as the value of the site was drastically reduced following the discovery that most of the land in the area could subside within 15 years, Moore and Brock finally finished trading. On his death, Thomas Moore bequeathed £31,055 (nearly £2m) to his family. He had one child, Alison Mary Moore (born 1900), who married George Shard, in China, in 1922.

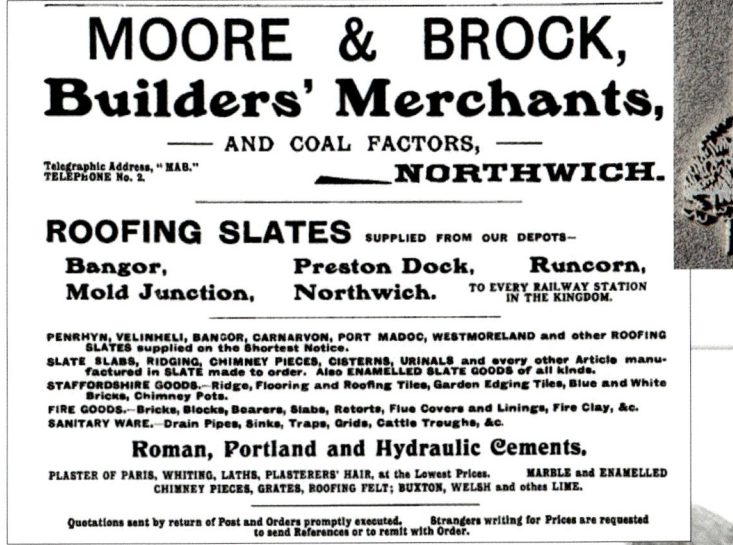

Above - A Moore and Brock advert from 1910. Above right - The M&B warehouse around the same time. Right - The Northwich Carrying Co. Ltd. at Baron's Quay, Northwich.

(COLIN) DEWI MORRIS

b. 1964

Dewi Morris is a former international, rugby union footballer, who played scrum half for the British Lions and England, achieving three caps for the former and 26 for the latter. Dewi lives with his wife, Penny, and their children, in The Bell House, Dalefords Lane, Sandiway.

The son of a Welsh father and an English mother, Dewi Morris was born and brought up in Crickhowell, Wales. Whilst at Crewe College he played rugby for Winnington Park, Northwich, before moving on to Liverpool St Helens and, finally, Orrell Rugby Union Football Club, Wigan, where he stayed for six years.

Dewi Morris in his England shirt at the height of his career.
Photo: © sporting-heroes.net

After only twelve games at St Helens Dewi got the "call up" for England, making his debut in 1988, against Australia, at Twickenham, when his try helped them to victory. He was dropped, in 1990, in favour of Richard Hill, but returned to the England team in 1992, and was selected for the British Lions side in 1993, for the New Zealand tour.

Dewi Morris retired from rugby union after the 1995 World Cup third place play-off match, against France, which he was disappointed to lose because they'd been unbeaten against the country for a long time. Sale RUFC enticed him out of retirement for a season, and they reached the final of the Pilkington Cup with no small thanks to Dewi's superb skill.

During his career, Dewi Morris played with some greats from the world of Rugby including Rob Andrew, Will Carling, Jeremy Guscott, Gavin and Scott Hastings and Rory and Tony Underwood. He now appears regularly, on *Sky Sports*, as a rugby union commentator with former England international, Stuart Barnes, and England and Lions centre, Will Greenwood.

Dewy launching Hartford High School's Run 2 Rio Day 2016.

SIR (WILLIAM) LEONARD OWEN

1897 - 1971

Sir Leonard Owen was an atomic engineer who lived, throughout most of his career, at The Dell on the A49 in Cuddington. He became Director of Engineering, at the Ministry of Atomic Energy Project, after the Second World War and, in 1957, took charge of the United Kingdom Atomic Energy Association (UKAEA). Leonard Owen was created a CBE in 1950, and received a Knighthood in the New Year's honours list for 1957. The University of Liverpool Archives hold a collection of items relating to him, the most notable of which is a manuscript diary kept whilst he was director of the Department of Atomic Energy Production. Sir Leonard's daily entries from 4th February 1946, until 30th August 1947, provide a valuable record of the early days of the UKAEA.

Sir (William) Leonard Owen in 1968.
Photo: ©National Portrait Gallery, London.

Leonard Owen's education, at the Liverpool Collegiate School, was interrupted in 1915, when he joined the 6th King's Liverpool Regiment and saw service in France. After WWI, he continued his engineering studies at Liverpool University and in 1922 joined Brunner Mond & Co. at Winnington, as a project engineer. When the company merged to form ICI, in 1926, there began a partnership with Christopher Hinton (later to be Lord Hinton, see page 43) which continued for thirty years.

With the approach of World War Two, both men were loaned to the Ministry of Supply and, in 1942, Leonard Owen became Director of the Royal Filling Factories. He was responsible for constructing the buildings, which were to be used for putting explosives into bombs and shells, and for keeping these structures abreast of the rapidly changing demands of the three fighting forces.

At the end of the war he agreed to join the industrial side of the Atomic Energy Project, as Director of Engineering, and during the next eleven years, Sir Leonard was an important part of major achievements in the new field of atomic technology, at the Springfields, Windscale, Capenhurst and Calder Hall plants. In 1957, until his retirement in 1962, Sir Leonard Owen took charge of the United Kingdom Atomic Energy Association Production group, as Authority Member for Production and Engineering.

To help them enjoy their final years, Sir Leonard and his wife built a house overlooking the Menai Strait in North Wales. They had an enduring friendship with Lord and Lady Hinton. Kenneth, the oldest of their two sons, also became an engineer with ICI at Winnington.

CHARLES NICHOLAS PAUL PHIPPS

1845 – 1913

Charles N. P. Phipps in 1880.

Charles N. P. Phipps was living at Gorstage Hall (page 5) in 1881 with his wife and eight "servants". He was a well known coffee merchant, a Conservative MP for Westbury (1880–1885) and High Sheriff of Wiltshire (1888).

Charles Phipps was the eldest son of Charles Paul Phipps (1815–1880) and Emma Mary Benson. Following his education, at Eton, he was sent to Brazil to work for the family firm, Phipps & Co, which exported coffee from Rio de Janeiro. In 1871, following the death of his uncle, John Lewis Phipps, he became a partner in the business. It was at this point that Charles came to live in Gorstage, as the firm's offices were in nearby Liverpool, but his principle home was Chalcot House, Westbury, Wiltshire, which had been owned by the Phipps family since 1585. Phipps and Co. was one of the largest British export houses for coffee in the world. It increased its volume from 91,000 bags of coffee in 1850 to half a million - valued at £2,000.000 (£180m) - by the mid 1870s

Chalcot House, Westbury.

At the 1880 general election, Phipps was elected as the Conservative Member of Parliament for Westbury. A petition by the defeated Liberal Party candidate (and outgoing MP), Abraham Laverton, to have his election annulled on the grounds of bribery, treating and undue influence, failed. He remained MP for Westbury until 1885. He was also a member of Wiltshire County Council and served as chairman of the Selection Committee from 1911 to 1913.

In 1874, he married Clara, the daughter of Sir Frederick H. Bathurst, of Clarendon Park, Wiltshire. They had one son and six daughters. Their second daughter, Norah Jacintha Phipps, married Sir John Fuller, 1st Baronet, of Neston Park, Wiltshire, and was the mother of Sir Gerard Fuller, 2nd Baronet. During their school holidays Charles welcomed the sons of the King of Siam to Chalcot and was rewarded with copious gifts of Thai silver. At his death, he left over £90,600 (£9.3m) to his widow. His younger brother, William Wilton Phipps, was the grandfather of Joyce Grenfell.

Norah Jacintha Phipps

Sir John Fuller, Charles Phipps' son-in-law.

Lucy Pierce in about 1947.

LUCY ELEANOR PIERCE

1884 - 1968

Lucy Eleanor Pierce was an accomplished pianist and Professor of Piano at the Royal Manchester College of Music. For over thirty years she was one of the most frequently broadcast pianists on the BBC Midland and Northern regional wavelengths, and gave many recitals in concert halls all over the UK. She was one of the founder members of the Manchester Contemporary Music Society and two of her pupils were the distinguished musicians, John Brennan and Ronald Stevenson.

Lucy's parents, William and Elizabeth, and her sisters, Annie and Ada, were all school teachers. Although born in Davenham, her family home until she moved to Sandiway, was the School House, Hartford. In the 1901 census, she was 16 and boarding at Hartington, Derbyshire, where she attended Derby High School for Girls. After her schooling, Lucy entered the Royal Manchester College of Music, where she studied under the legendary Egon Petri, and travelled to Germany and Austria for the Weimar and Vienna master classes, under Ferruccio Busoni. At college, she won the Dayas Gold Medal for her piano performances. In 1912 she returned to the RMCM as a member of their teaching staff, working with many notable names in the musical world such as Wilhelm Backhaus (piano), Arthur Catterall (violin and conductor), Carl Fuchs (cello), Geoffrey Gilbert (flute), Evelyn Rothwell (Lady Barbirolli, oboe) and Henry Holst (violin).

Lucy Pierce has been described, rather grandly, as "the doyenne of Manchester pedagogues". She certainly was a dedicated, and respected, senior piano teacher, until her death in the 1968. When she died, £1,000 (£20,800), and her splendid library of music, were bequeathed to the RMCM. and the annual "Lucy Pierce Award", for piano, was established. Lucy lived with her sister, Ada (who died in 1961), at Bryn Cottage, Weaverham Road, where Henry Holst, one time leader of the Berlin Philharmonic Orchestra, would often visit to play tennis. Locals remember her as a tall, friendly lady who enjoyed tending her garden.

After her death, Lucy Pierce's name was inscribed in the *Book of Remembrance* in The Friends of the Musician's Chapel in London.

ADAM PETER RICKITT

b. 1978

Adam Rickitt is the youngest of four sons born to Peter and Gillian Rickitt, of Pinfold Hollows, Cuddington. He is an actor, model, singer and charity fund raiser who rose to fame in the 1990s playing the part of Nick Tilsley in the ITV soap opera, Coronation Street. In 1999 he left the series, returning briefly in 2002, and for a longer spell from 2003 to 2004. His most controversial storyline was in 2003 when the character of Nick was involved in the series' first gay kiss. At the National Television Awards UK in 1998 and 1999 he was nominated the most popular newcomer. Adam is now part of the pop group "5th Story", an English super group consisting of 1990s to early 2000s pop stars, formed in 2013.

Adam Rickitt starred as Mark Cohen in the 2002 UK tour of the musical *Rent* before making a return to the London stage to star in Bill Kenwright's production, *Office Games*, followed by a new play, *Final Judgment*. In December 2006, Adam appeared in his first pantomime, *Cinderella*, in the role of Prince Charming at the Norwich Theatre Royal. He particularly enjoyed a spell with the cast of *Shortland Street*, in early 2007, as the mysterious Kieran Mitchell and said that he preferred this new role to that on *Coronation Street*. Adam also appeared in two other television series: *Doctors* and *Judge John Deed*.

When Adam left *Coronation Street,* in 1999, it was to start a musical career. He signed a six-album deal with Polydor, but only released one album: *Good Times*. Rickitt's first single, *I Breathe Again*, reached number five in the UK hit parade but follow up singles, *Everything My Heart Desires* and *Best Thing*, were less successful, reaching numbers 15 and 25 respectively. In 2014, he became part of the super group "5th Story", along with Kenzie from Blazin' Squad, Dane Bowers from Another Level, Kavana and Gareth Gates.

In an attempt to become a Conservative Party Candidate, Adam Rickitt made appearances on political shows such as *Question Time*, *Good Morning A.M.* with Andrew Marr, and as a guest reporter for the ITV breakfast television programme, *Daybreak*, covering international and local political functions. The RSPCA; Help Harry Help Others, the brain cancer charity; and the mental health foundation, Caerus Partnership; have all benefited from his support. His experiences, briefly as a child model, and subsequently modelling for UK magazines such as *Attitude* and *Cosmopolitan*, possibly led him to speak publicly about suffering from bulimia as a teenager and how male sufferers have largely been neglected. Adam Rickitt was educated at Sedbergh boarding school in Cumbria, gaining five A levels at the top grade but refused an offer from Cambridge University to study law because he wanted to become an actor. On December 21st 2014, he married *Good Morning Britain* reporter, Katie Fawcett.

DOMINIC JAMES RILEY

b. 1966

Dominic Riley

Dominic Riley moved to Cuddington in 1976 with his parents, Timothy and Mary Riley, and his sister and brother, Kate and Matthew. Their home was Barratwich, a cottage on Cuddington Lane, where Mary still lives with her second husband, Bernard Burton. The family are, rightly, very proud of Dominic who is an internationally renowned book restorer and fine binder. He undertakes work for institutions, book dealers and collectors, and examples of his bindings can be found in important, permanent collections in the USA and the UK, including the British Library and the Rylands Library in Manchester, the National Library of Wales, the Grolier Club in New York and the San Francisco Public Library.

Barratwich, the cottage on Cuddington Lane where Dominic was brought up.

Dominic has taught and lectured throughout Great Britain and Europe, America, Australia and New Zealand, with workshops and presentations in binderies, libraries and colleges. He is an accredited lecturer with the National Association of Decorative and Fine Art Societies (NADFAS). and was elected Fellow of Designer Bookbinders in 2008. He is Vice President of the Society of Bookbinders and co-founder of the Society of Bookbinders Seminar and the SoB and DB joint workshop series. He and his partner, Michael, spend part of each year teaching master classes in San Francisco and across the USA.

Dominic gained ten prizes in the Designer Bookbinders' Annual Competition between 2001 and 2007, including both first prizes and the Mansfield Silver Medal in 2007. The highlight of his career occurred when he won the top award of £10,000, known as the Paul Getty Prize, at the second Designer Bookbinders' International Bookbinding ceremony in 2013. Given the theme of William Shakespeare, Dominic produced a binding made of brown and black goatskin which depicted the story of *Pyramus and Thisbe* in a forest landscape, lit by the full moon, with the names of the lovers half hidden in the stars. Competition entrants represented 31 countries. His binding was

Pyramis and Thisbe, Dominic's winning entry at the Sir Paul Getty Bodleian Bookbinding ceremony 2013. The name of Shakespeare's play is spelt out in the stars.

acquired by the Bodleian Library in Oxford. Stephen Conway, President of Designer Bookbinders, said the competition had "moved bookbinding in new and exciting directions."

Michael Burke

Dominic was educated at St Monica's Catholic Primary School, Appleton, Warrington; St Nicholas High School, Hartford; Douai School in Berkshire, where he first learnt bookbinding from the Benedictine monks; and Leeds University (Art History and English), during which time he was apprenticed during the summer months to bookbinder Paul Delrue on the City Walls in Chester. He went on to study formally at the London College of Printing (1988-90).

In 1966, the devastating floods of the river Arno in Florence killed 101 people and damaged or destroyed millions of masterpieces of art and rare books. Dominic's teachers were part of this restoration project and his family see it as significant that his birthday coincides with the date of the floods.

After graduation, Dominic worked in London for a year, including the V&A, New York and San Francisco (1990-2001). In 1996, with Michael Burke, he co-founded the binding programme at the San Francisco Centre for the Book, and earned his living restoring rare books and teaching and lecturing at the University of California, and across the USA for the Guild of Bookworkers. He was elected President of the Hand Bookbinders of California and, with his friend and colleague, John DeMerritt, made a TV show, *The Book Boys*. Since 2001, Dominic has lived in the Lake District where he has a bindery with Michael, also a bookbinder, who specialises in paper conservation. Below are examples of Dominic's wonderful bindings:

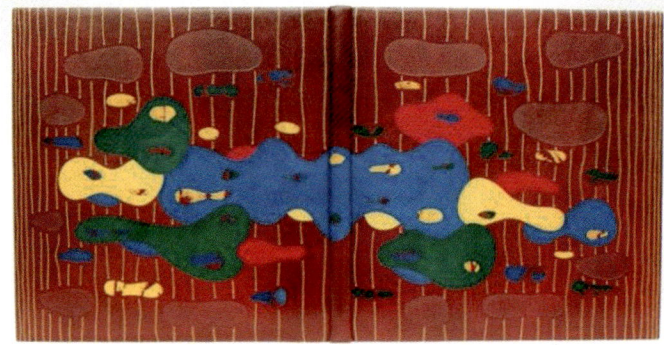

***The Waste Land* by T.S. Eliot**

This is a very large book from the famous Arion Press of San Francisco. The design is an abstracted view of the landscape in ruins. The cover is full brick red goatskin with solid and feathered onlays of red, blue, yellow and green goatskin with gold tooled lines and impressed shapes. It has leather joints and doublures, and impressed suede, and additional painted paper, flyleaves.

Water

A book of poems and images on the theme of water. The design was inspired by the constant rain in the Lake District. It is in the 'Tudor style', developed by Paul Delrue, one of Dominic's early mentors. It consists of overlaying strips of leather and the whole is tooled with silver.

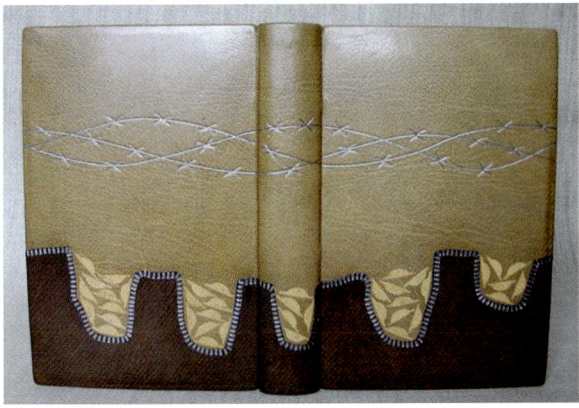

The Somme: An Eyewitness History

The three overpowering motifs of The Battle are depicted: the trenches, the helmets and the barbed wire. Pewter tooling is used for the wire and the bullets which edge the trenches. It is bound in light and dark brown goatskin. This binding won the Mansfield Silver Medal in 2007

The Dead by James Joyce

This book is bound in black goatskin with a painted top edge, leather doublures and suede fly leaves. The panels are worked off the book, with sanded onlays and sharply inscribed blind lines, lightly sanded and waxed.

Gilead by Marilynne Robinson

The inspiration for the design comes from the quote "an impressive sun shines on us all", and is represented by the radiating gold lines on the cover, and a sun image which appears on the painted fore-edge. A bloodstain on the bottom painted edge and on the small onlay on the front cover references the civil war. The shapes on the cover are the abstracted outlines of the states of Kansas and Iowa.
For its binding Dominic used medium brown goatskin, back-pared feathered onlays and gold tooling.

Some Birds and Beasts and their Feasts by Enid Marx

This book can be found in a collection in the Rylands Library, Manchester.
The binding is purple goatskin, multi-coloured onlays, painted edges, leather doublures and suede flyleaves. The gold tooled dots depict the fanciful, abstracted images of mythical birds. The doublures have more depictions of imaginary beasts.

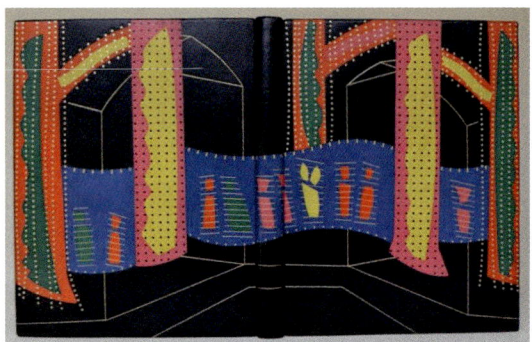

A Midsommer Night's Dream by William Shakespeare

Bound in black goatskin with multi-coloured onlays and gold tooling, the arches of the palace and the forest are set within the space of the theatre. The protagonists are depicted across the banner which

Sonnets by Richard Barnfield

A sumptuous mustard goatskin was used for this binding with brown, blue, and green goatskin onlays.

Dominic Riley's publications include: *Gold Leaf* (Hand Bookbinders of California); *Ampersand* (Pacific Centre for the Book Arts); *Bookbinder* (Society of Bookbinders); *The New Bookbinder* (Design Bookbinders) and several articles for the *Biblio* and *Illustrator* magazines. He also presented the film, *Seventy Years in Bookbinding: a Portrait of Bernard Middleton,* in 2008.

Dominic says of his chosen profession:

"I enjoy all aspects of bookbinding, from restoration to teaching and Design Binding. Restoration is hugely challenging, and is surgical in its approach. Teaching is about giving back, but it also keeps the craft alive. If you have a passion, you must pass it on. Design Binding is the way we get to be artists, but is also the most mentally taxing. I have created forty or so Design Bindings since 2001, and now make about eight a year."

Pictured left to right are Emma (Dominic's niece), Kate (his sister), Mary (his mother), Dominic, Bernard (Mary's second husband), Clare (Mary's sister), Nick (Kate's husband) and Michael Burke (Dominic's partner).

Right - a charming photo of Dominic with his nephew, Harry. Left - Dominic in his workshop.

JOHN ARTHUR SANER

1865 - 1952

Col. Saner was clearly proud of his military career.

On the opposite side of the road to St John's Church, Sandiway, there is a long drive, at the end of which stands Toolerstone House, the home of Colonel John Arthur Saner, from about 1910 until 1932. John Saner was one of the outstanding engineers of his generation who gained inter-national acclaim for his innovative use of electricity to power swing bridges and, most famously, The Anderton Boat Lift.

From 1888 until 1934 John Saner was Chief Engineer for Weaver Navigation. In this role he designed and supervised the construction of seven bridges. The Hayhurst and Town Bridges in Northwich (built in 1888 and 1889), were constructed to float on pontoons, to combat the subsidence due to the extraction of salt beneath the town, and are believed to be the two earliest electronically operated swing bridges in Britain. Three other swing bridges were at Sutton Weaver, near Frodsham (1923), Acton Bridge (1932) and Winnington (1909). The Sutton Weaver bridge had a £4.5 million makeover in 2014. Smaller "Saner" creations were The Riversdale footbridge (1930), and the Dutton Horse Bridge (1919), which is now recorded in the National Heritage List for England as Grade II listed.

The first boat lift at Anderton was designed by Edward Clark and opened to traffic in 1875. It lifted and lowered vessels the fifty feet between the River Weaver, and the Trent and Mersey Canal above, but Victorian technology was not quite up to the rigours of salt polluted water found in this part of Cheshire, and the metalwork soon corroded. Col. John Saner was asked to find a solution, and in 1904 he proposed replacing the hydraulic rams with electric motors and a system of pulleys and counterweights so that the caissons (two huge watertight tanks, each with sealable doors) could carry boats up and down independently. All the workings would be above ground which would mean easy maintenance and a longer working life. Work began on the lift in 1906 and Saner vowed that, although a major conversion was needed in the form of a substantial new super structure over the original lift, the rebuild would take two years and only need to be closed for three short spells. This involved a marvellous feat of engineering, planning and execution but, under the watchful eye of Col. Saner, all went smoothly and the work was completed, as promised, in 1908.

Colonel Saner was the oldest of ten children born to John and Mary Saner in Kingston-upon-Hull, Yorkshire. His early education was completed as a boarder at The Common School, Woolwich. On 21st March 1890, John became a Member of the Institute of Mechanical Engineers and in 1892 married Ethel Maude Jameson. They had three children: John, Ethel and Phyllis, who were all born at John and Ethel's first home together: Highfield, Castle, Northwich.

There are several Saner publications including, *Swing bridges over the Weaver Navigation* (1929), and copies of the many lectures and reports he gave throughout his life. In 1943, he came out of retirement to give a detailed report for the Ministry of War Transport, proposing a waterway from Weaver Navigation to Wolverhampton. It was something Col. Saner had worked on while in office and his successor supported him in the ensuing years but, ultimately, nothing was done. In 1932 he built himself a new home, Sandiway Heyes, in Hartford. The original build shows unstinting attention to detail and high grade building materials were used throughout. It is here that John Arthur Saner passed away, in 1952, leaving £25,725 (nearly £0.75m).

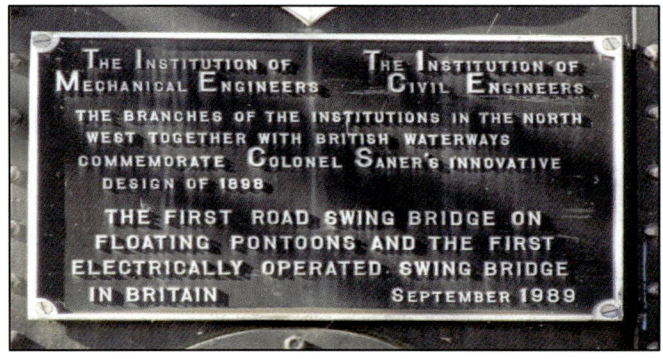

Top left - This plaque is to commemorate John Saner's invention of the first road swing bridge on floating pontoons and the first electronically operated swing bridge in Britain. It is to be found on the Town Bridge leading into The Bull Ring, Northwich. Above is "The Anderton Boat Lift Mural" depicting "The People who made it Happen: Edward Clark, Sir Edward Williams and Col. John Saner". To the right from the top are pictured: Town Bridge, The Hayhurst Bridge, Sutton Weaver Bridge, Acton Bridge, Winnington Bridge, The Riverside Footbridge and Dutton Horse Bridge.

The Anderton Boat Lift, Lift Lane, Northwich, is Col. Arthur Saner's most outstanding achievement. The Canal and River Trust describe it as "an incredible edifice, perched on the banks of the River Weaver Navigation like a giant three-storey-high iron spider... . No description can adequately convey the sheer scale of this engineering feat. " Now classified as an historic monument, a National Lottery grant of three and a half million pounds made possible its restoration and reopening in 2002, by Prince Charles.

Toolerstone, the home of Colonel Saner in Sandiway. It was renovated extensively by him in 1913. Prior to that it had been known as Toolerstone Farm (page 108). Nowadays it is called Toolerstone House.

CLIFFORD SCHWABE

1874 - 1946

Clifford Schwabe lived at Cuddington Grange, Norley Road, until his death in 1947. He was the son of Louis and Blanche Schwabe of Hart Hill Estate, Salford, and was a direct descendent of William the Conqueror. Louis was a well known silk and embroidery manufacturer in Portland Street, Manchester, and printed some of the fabric for Queen Victoria's wedding dress. Clifford appears to have eventually gone into the family's textile business, but there was also a close family connection between the Schwabes and Gustav Wolf who founded the Harland and Wolf Ship Building Company (Gustave Wolf married Fanny Schwabe) and there is a record of Clifford starting at the shipyard as a "gentleman apprentice" on Monday 23rd June 1890. Their most famous ship was the Titanic. When he died, in 1922, Louis Schwabe left £323,826 (£14.15m) to be divided between Clifford and his two brothers.

Clifford Schwabe, on the right, on a visit to Canada to see his cousin and his wife, Gilbert and Sara, in the mid 1940s.

Clifford Schwabe was lucky to have survived childhood. On returning from work one day his father came across his three sons fighting for their lives in the icy water they had fallen into whilst skating on a lake. He saved all three but Clifford was unconscious when pulled from the water and needed lengthy medical attention. He married May Littledale, the youngest daughter of the late J. B. Littledale (page 107), on 12th August 1913, at St John's Church, Chester. At the time, Clifford was living at Arden, Ashley, Altrincham, and that is where the couple set up home. Two daughters followed: Maud and Betty. The former married Antony Ronald Legard, nicknamed "Loopy", an Indian-born English cricketer who played 36 first-class matches for Oxford University and Worcestershire and, aged forty, made a one off appearance for the MCC, against Ireland, in Dublin. Clifford Schwabe was a member of the Manchester Polo Club, a forerunner of the Cheshire Polo Club, and won creditable medals in WWI. He died on the 9th November 1946, leaving £53,878 (£1.75m) to Henry Thackeray Schwabe. His family home, Hart Hill, was sold to Salford City in 1925, and demolished two years later.

Cuddington Grange today. For an idea of how the house would have looked in the days of Clifford Schwabe see page 105.

MARGARET SHERRY

b. 1946

Margaret Sherry, at home in Croft House, with her Jack Russell, Michael.

Margaret Sherry is an artist living in a charming John Douglas house in Sandiway. She has lived there for almost 40 years and works from home in a sunny studio overlooking her much loved garden. Many years ago Margaret made the decision to market her own artwork and formed a limited company. Her work is varied in subject matter from detailed architectural buildings, botanical illustrations, to cats riding bicycles produced mainly in watercolour and pencil.

After university Margaret produced illustrations for children's books, advertising, greetings cards, stamps, stickers, cross stitch and magazines. She writes "I am often asked how I achieved success in such a difficult area; the secret is to be persistent, have vast energy and enthusiasm along with the love of relentless hard work! Also the ability to draw whatever you are asked to produce in double quick time! I am self motivated. I need to manage my own time, living an exhausting social life woven around 'work'. If I want to weed the garden all afternoon and paint until 3am there is no one to say otherwise!"

St John's, Sandiway

Croft House, Sandiway

Her four children have grown up in Sandiway and are extremely successful in their chosen careers. They have all come back to live and work in Cheshire bringing, as Margaret says "...the joy of grandchildren. I see them all on different days, throughout the week, when we cook, chat and laugh together. The boys and my energetic Jack Russell, Michael, play football... I don't!" Margaret is often seen in the village walking Michael and making quick pencil sketches of houses, trees and other interesting canines.

A small selection of Margaret's enchanting and often humorous designs for greetings cards. Left to right: Out of Control!!!, Butterflies on Apples, Christmas Watering Can, Hedgehog and Toadstools and Plagues.

Below are three paintings of local interest: St John's, Sandiway; No. 2 Hadrian Way; and a watercolour of Margaret's home, Croft House, completed after a fall of snow.

THOMAS NEIL SHERRY

b. 1970

Tom Sherry has produced many drama series for television including *New Tricks*, *Murphy's Law* and *Scott & Bailey*. Currently he is executive producer at Red Production Company based in Media City, Salford. Tom lives with his family in Willington, Kelsall, but grew up at Croft House, Sandiway. He is the son of Margaret Sherry (page 73)

Tom Sherry

Tom has been BAFTA (British Acadamy of Film and Television Arts) nominated for *Murphy's Law*, *Scott & Bailey* and *Prey*, and received an EMMY nomination for *New Tricks* which starred a whole host of famous names including James Bolam, Amanda Redman, Denis Waterman and Nicholas Lyndhurst. Tom won the Royal Television Society award for *Burn it*.

At the age of 14 Tom was cast as an extra in a television commercial. This had a profound effect on deciding his career. After university, he worked within the TV industry as an assistant director, and a location and production manager, on a variety of feature films and television dramas, including *In The Name of the Father*, *Far From the Madding Crowd*, *Cracker*, *Sherlock Holmes*, and *Queer as Folk*. Recent productions have included *Ordinary Lies* and *Paranoid*.

Neil says of his home county:

"Cheshire is such a lovely county and I'm very fortunate to live there with my extended family who all live close by. I am delighted that my own family are growing up there and experiencing many of the delights I did as a boy. Working in the Northwest, championing all it has to offer and sharing it with those not privileged to be Northern, is something I'm enormously proud of. If ever there are days when you need to get things into perspective, go for a run or a walk in Delamere Forest or along the Whitegate Way, and you'll know how blessed we are."

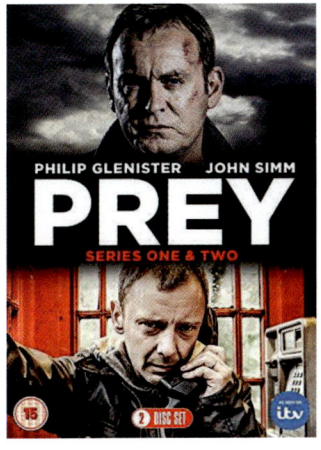

The front of *Prey*'s DVD shows the series two stars - Philip Glenister (above) and John Simm (below). John plays Detective Sergeant Marcus Farrow. The two series play out as two three-part stories covering two criminal cases. It has been televised in the UK and in the US.

FRANCES SEBA SMITH

b. 1935

Frances Seba Smith at work in her art studio at Abbotsford.

Frances Seba Smith is an artist and printmaker who has lived and worked at Abbotsford, Cuddington, (page 83) for 49 years. She has work in private and public collections at the Grosvenor Museum, Chester; the Museum of Fine Art, Malta; Great Universal Stores Head Office, London; both British Midland Airlines and Chepstow House in Manchester and the Masterworks Foundation, Bermuda. Although Frances has taught in several colleges and run courses from her Abbotsford studio, in drawing, painting and printmaking, she now concentrates on her own work. She has exhibited widely in Britain, Malta, Canada, Russia, Italy, France, Germany and Bermuda.

Frances was born in Montreal, Canada, where she studied at Ecole des Beaux Arts, gaining a diploma in Publicity. After graduating, she worked for the Sun Life Company, Canada, as a graphic designer responsible for their sales promotions and won three awards for her advertising material. In 1982, Frances Seba Smith gained a First Class Honours Degree in Fine Arts from North Staffordshire University, specialising in printmaking. In 1990, at Abbotsford, she set up a studio, with both an antique Albion press and an etching press; here she makes relief, mono and etching prints in a variety of media.

Frances Seba Smith has devoted much time and effort promoting art in the community. She usually opens her studio to the public for the Cheshire Open Studios each September and, for many years, served on the Patrons Committee at Manchester Art Gallery. Frances is a founder member of Cheshire Artists Network, a member of the Manchester Academy of Fine Arts and has been made an honorary retired board member of Norton Priory Museum.

Travelling has given Frances Seba Smith constant inspiration for her work. She was an artist in residence at the Casa Piccalo in Malta, and the Masterworks Foundation, Bermuda, with large successful exhibitions at the end of the residencies. She writes that her creativity,

"...is based on drawing and photography, taking images into paint and print with the exciting diversification that entails".

Further information about France Seba Smith's work can be found in these publications:

Picturesque Chester: The City in Art - Peter Broughton.
International Dictionary of Artists who have Painted Malta - Nicholas de Piro KM.
A Colourful Canvas, Twelve Northwest Women Artists - Wendy Levy and Judith Rose.

On the next page are some examples of Frances Seba Smith's stunning paintings and prints:

Boats on the Beach, Rhosneigr. Oil on canvas.

View From the Hill. Print on paper.

Along the Bank. Oil on canvas.

Blues. Monoprint on paper.

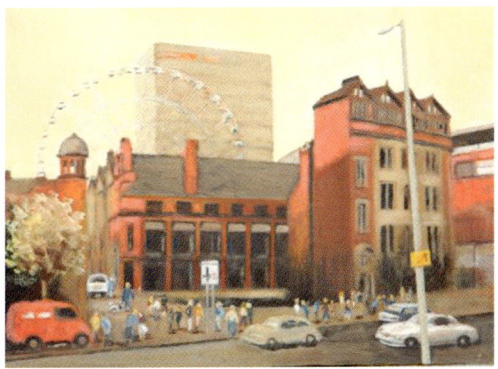
The Wheel Manchester. Oil on board.

The Rock. Etching on paper.

Bella and Louis. Oil on canvas.

Chester Library. Linoprint.

SHIRLEY ELAINE STRONG

b. 1958

Shirley Strong competing for Great Britain in the World Championships in 1983.
Photo: ©sporting-heroes.net

Shirley Strong is known by everyone in the Northwich area as the Cuddington girl who won a silver medal for Great Britain at the 1984 Summer Olympics in Los Angeles. She only lost out on the gold by 0.04 seconds; Benita Fitzgerald-Brown of the United States winning in 12.84. Shirley was also the gold medallist at the Commonwealth Games in Brisbane, Australia, in 1982. At the height of her career she was among the most popular athletes in the UK with a public who regarded her as "one of us" as she admitted to going "out on the town" and enjoying herself. Born on Grange Road, Cuddington, on 18th November 1958, and the daughter of Don and Sheila Strong, she attended Northwich Grammar School for Girls, Leftwich, and remained in the village throughout her athletic career.

When Shirley Strong began competing nationally, she gained two second places in the 100 metres hurdles at the 3 A's and the UK Athletics Championships in 1977, and again in 1978. Between 1979 and 1984 she won six consecutive golds at the 3 A's and was UK Champion in 1979, 1980 and 1983. Her first major championship was the 1978 Commonwealth Games, in Edmonton, Canada, where she won the silver medal. This was followed, in 1983, by a creditable fifth place at the World Championships; Great Britain's highest placing in the event until Tiffany Porter finished in fourth place in 2011. A boycott of the Olympic Games in Los Angeles, by the eastern European countries, meant that she went into the 100 metres hurdles final as favourite but she claimed that put tremendous pressure on her and for her rival, Benita Fitzgerald-Brown, it was, literally, the race of her life.

Shirley Strong, in Lane 7, about to win a silver medal in the 100-metre hurdles at the 1984 Summer Olympics in the Los Angeles Memorial Coliseum, California. Photo: ©Sporting-heroes.net

In the years following Los Angeles, Shirley Strong was frequently troubled by problems with her Achilles tendon and, after competing in the 1987 indoor season, she retired from athletics. Now known by her married name, Shirley Holloway, she has two daughters and lives in Holmes Chapel, Cheshire.

PETER JOHN SUMMERS

b. 1929

Peter Summers moved into Delamere Manor (page 8) after Edward Graham-Wood's departure in 1967. He was the great grandson of the founder of John Summers and Sons, a major United Kingdom iron and steel producer, based at Shotton, Flintshire.

An old advert for John Summers and Sons steelworks, Shotton.

Peter Summers in 2011

John Summers started the firm in Bolton, making nails to fasten the metal strips on to clogs. By 1909, it was the largest manufacturer of galvanised steel in the country. In 1920 the firm built 300 homes for its workers, known as Garden City, and during WW2 Summers produced 3,350,000 tons of steel ingots and rolled 2,220,000 tons of sheets. At its peak, in the 1960s, they employed more than 13,000. All the Summers sons, and their sons, were "Iron Masters". Peter's Great Uncle Frank left £206,084 (over £11m) in 1926 and his Great Uncle James employed 500 hands as far back as 1881.

The son of Sir Richard Summers, Peter joined the works in 1954. He was not allowed to become identified with one department but had to maintain an objectivity and distance that would enable him to take an overall view of the family business. In 1967, steel was nationalised and Peter was the only member of the Summers clan to remain at Shotton as personnel director for the Scottish and North-West Group of British Steel. It was Peter who managed the successful, early phases of the development of Deeside Industrial Park. He was mentioned in parliament for creating 8,000 jobs. Employees from the time hold Peter in high regard and today's prosperous and flourishing Deeside is the legacy of Peter Summers and his predecessors. Peter now lives with his wife, Gillian, in Little Budworth.

The John Summers headquarters, on the river Dee, is now a listed building.

John Summers, the founder of the Shotton works and great grandfather of Peter Summers.

JULIE SUMMERS

b.1960

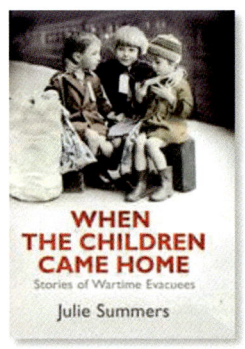

Julie Summers shown here with her Border Terriers who, she says, "keep me entertained and fit. They sleep in two old wine boxes under the window in my office".
Photo: barkerevans.com

Julie Summers was born on the Wirral near Liverpool but brought up at Delamere Manor, Cuddington. She is the daughter of Peter and Gillian Summers (page 79). Julie is an author, biographer, historian and broadcaster, particularly known for her book, *Jambusters*, a remarkable story which inspired the ITV drama *Home Fires*. After obtaining a joint honours degree in German and History of Art at Bristol University, Julie spent twenty years working in the art world. Her final position was as Head of Exhibitions at the Ashmolean Museum, Oxford, 2000-2004, but "inexorably" she was drawn towards writing for which she has a passion. In 2004 she became a full time author.

On her website Julie notes: "I have a little study in the attic of our house with one of the best views in Oxford – the dreaming spires seen from Iffley. I write in the mornings and find the problem is not sticking to the routine but tearing myself away from writing at the end of the day... I describe myself as a biographer and historian but the most important thing for me is to be a story teller."

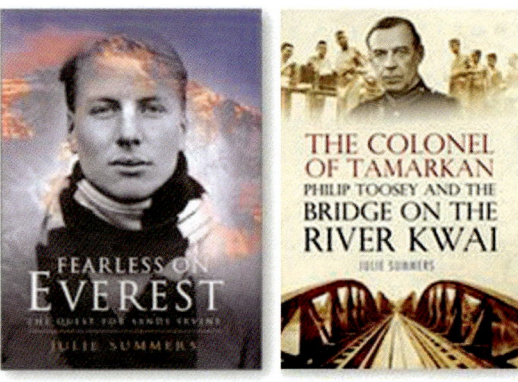

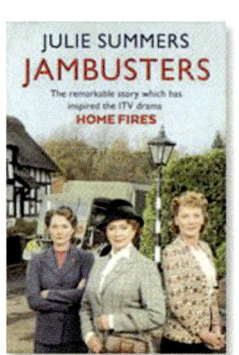

Julie is particularly interested in the way people in the past coped in extreme situations and her books shown here, covering WW2, rowing, mountaineering and exploration, reflect this interest. The two books above are particularly poignant to Julie. Sandy Irvine, on the left, was her Great Uncle. He failed to return from Everest in 1924. Philip Toosey, on the right, was her maternal Grandfather. Brigadier Sir Philip Toosey was the British CO in charge of the Bridge on the River Kwai PoW camp in Thailand. He was immortalised in the eponymous film. Julie says "...he was a fabulous man and a great character."

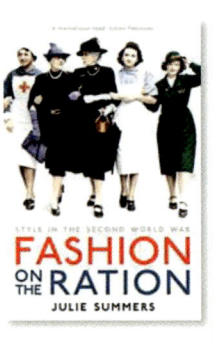

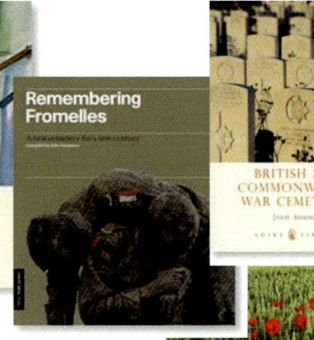

EDWARD TAYLEUR

1821 - 1891

At the time of the 1851 census, a trio of interesting gentlemen were residing at Pemberton Cottage (now Portobello, page 9). Lawrence Peel and Edward Tayleur were joint tenants and Fred Peel, Lawrence's brother, was a visitor.

Charles Tayleur

After the death of his father, Charles Tayleur, in the 1860s, Edward Tayleur inherited The Vulcan Foundry, Newton-le-Willows, and Bank Quay Foundry, Warrington. The firm became Edward Tayleur and Co. Edward, a civil engineer from Walton, Lancashire, had joined his father's locomotive building firm at Newton-le-Willows, in 1843. Charles was one of the chief industrial magnates of his age, besides owning extensive lands and properties in England and Wales (including 10,000 acres in Pembrokeshire). Charles Tayleur's Vulcan factory constructed several of the earliest and greatest locomotives, employing 620 men and 98 boys. Robert Stevenson, who designed the famous "Rocket" locomotive, was a partner in the firm for several years. In 1847, Charles and his son, Edward, entered into partnership with George Sanderson and took over Bank Quay Foundry in Warrington, a firm with the facilities for building steam and sailing ships of iron.

Under the Tayleur's stewardship, the Bank Quay Foundry won an award at the 1851 Great Exhibition held at the Crystal Palace in London for their "Great Hydraulic Press" which was used the following year to raise the tubes of the Britannia Bridge over the Menai Strait. In 1853, "The largest iron vessel ever built in Lancashire was launched from the yard of Messrs Tayleur & Co., Bank Quay Foundry". She was named *RMS Tayleur*, after the Tayleur family and was chartered by the White Star Line.

RMS *Tayleur*, described as "the first Titanic", was a fully rigged iron clipper- large, fast and technically advanced, but she ran aground and sank on her maiden voyage, in 1854. Of more than 650 aboard, only 290 survived. Several books have been written telling the story.

Built at the Vulcan Foundry in 1871, this was the first locomotive to run in Japan.

At Newton-le-Willows, locomotive building continued apace with significant developments in steam locomotion. Two thirds went abroad to countries as far away as India, America, New Zealand and Peru. Vulcan became renowned for the excellence of their materials and construction, with many examples outlasting the products of rival companies.

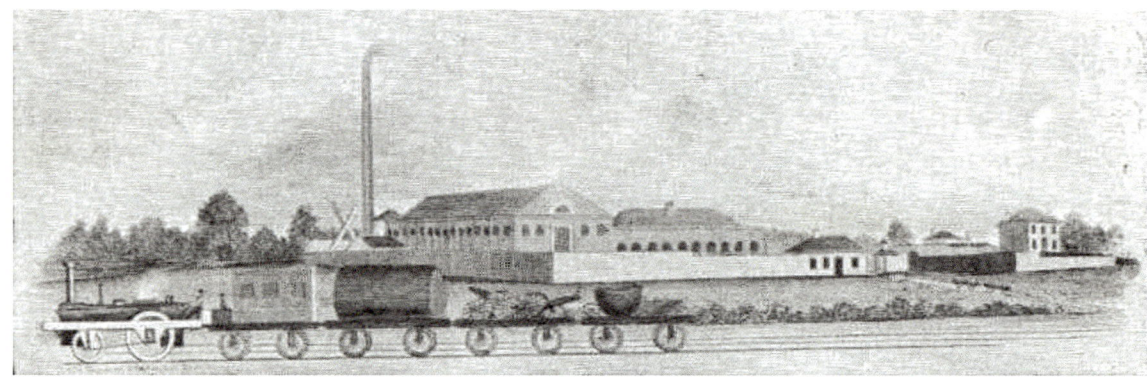

Above - An old print of Charles Tayleur's foundry dating from 1840, just three years before Edward Tayleur joined his father's firm. To the left is a drawing of the first locomotive to be built at the Vulcan Foundry. It was named *Tayleur* after the Tayleur family.

Lane's History of Newton-in-Makerfield, gives Edward Tayleur Esq. as Chairman of the local board of Improvement Commissioners from 1857 to 1863. By 1881 Edward had retired to Troqueer in Scotland as a farmer with 154 acres and ten employees. He married Marion Frances Kenyon but died without issue in 1891. Although he was known to have been a wealthy man, the details of his will are sealed. Soon after Edward's retirement the 1,000th locomotive trundled off the Newton-le-Willows production line.

LAWRENCE AND FRED PEEL (1806 - 1866 and 1818 -1867) were brothers, sons of the Rev'd Frederick Peel, rector of Willingham, Lincolnshire, and Canon of Lincoln Cathedral. He was the cousin of the highly influential statesman and Prime Minister, the Rt. Hon. Sir Robert Peel. Lawrence was an "attorney-at-law" with Miller, Peel, Hughes and Co., 6 Percy Buildings, Eberle Street, Liverpool, and Fred Peel was a merchant with the East India Company. The gentlemen died within a year of each other and each left £14,000 (£1.2m).

Sir Robert Peel, Prime Minister of Great Britain and great Uncle to Lawrence and Fred Peel.
Photo: ©National Portrait Gallery, London

THE THOMPSONS

The Thompsons were an important Cuddington family. They built some of the finest houses in the village and owned prosperous salt and brick works in Northwich. It was John Thompson (1790-1867) who established the various businesses and on his death they were divided between the family. Four of his descendents, Jabez Thompson, his youngest son, and three of his grandsons, Henry Ingram, Alfred Jabez and George Newton Thompson, built, between them: Abbotsford, Beechfield, Merlewood and The Hunting Box in Cuddington, and The Oaklands in Gorstage.

JABEZ THOMPSON (1838 - 1911), inherited the extensive Terracotta Brickworks on Manchester Road, Northwich. They produced common, fine and moulded bricks, and specialised in terracotta, ornamental pieces and panels. Examples of their work are to be found in London, Birmingham and all over the North West. Locally, Jabez Thompson's brickworks produced the decorative screen behind the altar at St Michael and All Saints Church, Little Leigh, which depicts Leonardo de Vinci's *Last Supper,* and two large carved panels on the front of the former Verdin Technical School and Gymnasium, Winsford. The Thompson stamp has been found on a lion's head unearthed in a garden in Northwich, and in the demolition of tracery windows at the Methodist Chapel, Poyser Street, Wrexham. A bust of John Ruskin, who is known to have visited Winnington Hall, is also thought to belong to the brickworks. It is now held by the Albert Hall Museum.

The Jabez Thompson 'Terracotta Brickworks' stamp found on items throughout the country.

Abbotsford today, designed by John Douglas for Jabez Thompson in 1890.

In 1890, Jabez Thompson built Abbotsford, on Warrington Road, naming it after the home of his favourite writer, Sir Walter Scott. Jabez lived there until his death. He was a member of the Northwich Board of Guardians, who looked after the welfare of the poor in the town, a stalwart supporter of the Temperance Movement and, in 1895, was elected as the first chairman of Cuddington Parish Council. He was well respected in the district. At his funeral 35 of his workers paid their respects by walking in front of the cortege from Hartford Hill to Davenham Parish Church. Jabez Thompson is commemorated, with his wife Sarah Edwards, on a plaque in St John's Church, Sandiway. The following page gives a selection of Jabez Thompson and Sons impressive, ornamental, terracotta work.

Jabez Thompson (left) with his brother, Ebenezer, outside Abbotsford. Photo: Mark Bevan Collection

These "Thompson" frieze bricks had somehow found their way to Germany, where they were recently for sale.

Left and above - Decoration around the entrance to the old Town hall, Widnes. The terracotta work for this Grade II listed building was all done by Jabez Thompson's brickworks.

Above - Leonardo de Vinci's *Last Supper*, the decorative screen behind the altar at St Michael and All Saints Church, Little Leigh.

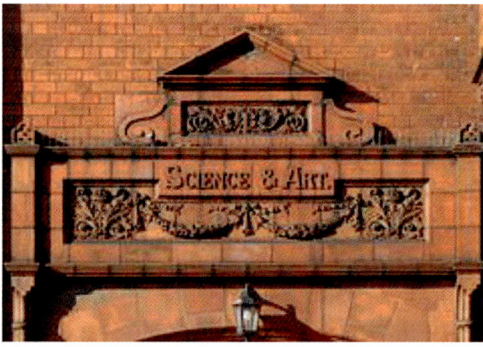

Decorative bricks found with the Jabez Thompson stamp, in a house in Southport.

A pair of stoneware lions, unusual for Mr Thompson.

Top, middle and bottom - Decorative detail by the Jabez Thompson's brickworks for the Verdin Technical School, Winsford.

The advert above, from the beginning of the twentieth century, makes interesting reading. Jabez Thompson certainly knew how to sell a product, although whether his "Thin White Partition" was ever actually patented has still to be proved. Recently, examples of the Brickwood have been found at Bridge House, Northwich, and Croich Hey House, Hawkshaw, Bury. At Bridge House each piece is stamped with "Jabez Thompson Patent Brickwood" and at Croich Hey, "Thompson's Patent. Terrawode Fixing Block, Northwich". It is thought that the blocks were used particularly for their fire and soundproofing qualities. The Northwich dwelling's partitioning was positioned between wooden panelling, and in Bury it was constructed between the Master bedroom and the servants quarters. Croich Hey was built for Fred Whowell and has other terracotta features which may well be by Jabez Thompson. In the advertisement, the gentleman posing to the right could well be Jabez himself or A. J. Thompson, as he was renowned for his particularly smart dress (page 87).

As this letter heading from 1910 shows, although Jabez Thompson's brickworks was sold in 1895, the purchaser, a Mr Molyneux, kept the "Thompson" name.

Henry Ingram Thompson
Photo: Mark Bevan Collection

HENRY INGRAM THOMPSON (1851 - 1937) lived at Beechfield on Forest Road, Cuddington (page 54). The salt working industry in the Northwich area, in the 19th and early 20th century, was on a much greater scale than anywhere else in Britain and Henry Thompson owned the Lion Salt Works, Marston.

In 1856 Henry's father, John Thompson Jr, and his grandfather, John Thompson Sr, had constructed the Alliance Salt Works in Marston, but in 1888 the Salt Union took over Northwich's salt industry in order to stem the intense rivalry between firms and stabilize prices. A disagreement ensued as to the Thompson families roles for the future. The Thompsons decided to sell the Alliance Works to the Salt Union and Henry Ingram and his father dug a new brine shaft adjacent to it, running it as an independent concern. The Lion Salt Works, as it was named, went from strength to strength. Henry took over its management when his father died in 1899 and an inventory, created in that year, valued the Lion Salt Works at £6,600 (£600,000).

By 1900, three fine open pan houses, used for making common salt by evaporation, had been constructed, together with stove houses, a brine tank, smithy, salt store, office, and four common or fishery pans used for making coarse salt. The interests of two other salt works belonging to Henry Ingram, that of Island and Willow Bank, Winsford, and Witton Hall, Northwich, were also sold to the Salt Union for £30,000 (nearly £3m). Orders were sent from Northwich, by narrow-boat and barge, to docks at Manchester and Merseyside to ship to overseas markets. Accounts studied for the period 1914-1918, show salt from the Lion Salt Works was dispatched to Africa, India, Australia, New Zealand, France, Vladivostok (Russia) and New York, and Guatemala in America. Trade is also known to have occurred with Belgium, Holland and Germany.

The Lion Salt Works remained in the Thompson family's hands through five generations. It ceased trading in 1986 and was left to deteriorate, but a Heritage Lottery Fund award of £5.29m meant that it has been possible to restore it to the glory of the Thompson days. The site is now a scheduled, listed monument, and includes the buried remains of the Alliance Works.

The restored Lion Salt Works, Marston.

In 1888 Henry Ingram Thompson bought Cuddington Grange, Norley Road (page 105), but as his wife, Emily Kinsey, did not like the house they never lived there. Instead Henry built Beechfield, where they resided for the rest of their lives. By 1896 he had also completed The Hawthorns, semi-detached houses on the White Barn crossroads, for his "servants".

ALFRED JABEZ THOMPSON (1858 - 1942) owned the Alliance White Salt Works, Marston, and appears to have been willing to run the works even with the Salt Union in control. After the Alliance's shaft collapsed, in 1898, it ceased operation and the site passed from the Salt Union into the ownership of Imperial Chemical Industries (ICI), who retained the salt rights. Despite this, Alfred or "A.J.", as he was known, was still said to be the power behind the family's salt enterprise and, furthermore, was reputed to be the, "best dressed man on the 9.06 business man's train from Cuddington to Manchester".

Merlewood as it appears today.

"A.J." married Emily Horner, the daughter of William Horner (page 47) and by 1900 the pair were settled in their newly built home, Merlewood, in Mill Lane, where they stayed for the rest of their married life. Merlewood is an imposing residence, standing in 19 landscaped acres. Alfred also built The Oaklands (Gorstage). He was an active JP, concerned, as his Uncle Jebez had been, about the needy youngsters of Northwich. Colin Lynch, a leading authority on the history of the town, writes that it was "A.J." who instigated and paid for the first "Free Meals" for poor children in the district, "which made their little faces beam with gladness" (*Colin Lynch's Northwich*, 2004).

James Edwin Thompson

Another of John Thompson, Jr's sons was **JAMES EDWIN THOMPSON** (1863 – 1927) who studied medicine and then emigrated to Galveston, USA, where he became Texas's first Professor of Surgery.

Poor resources meant the future appeared bleak when James Thompson first arrived in the US, but it did not stifle his spirits. He said of the time, that the burden he had to carry was heavy, and the creation of a school of medicine which would, "live up to the high standards of teaching to which we aspire", would require years of toil, individual sacrifice and united effort. During 36 years of considerable dedication, James Thompson became one of the country's most distinguished surgeons, and contributed more than 75 publications to the literature of surgery, dealing with such topics as the diagnosis and treatment of hepatic cancer, appendicitis, tumours of the face and neck, cleft palate and kidney malformations.

James Thompson married Eleanor Waters Roeck on May 16th 1896, and they became the parents of four daughters and four sons. The latter all received medical degrees from the University of Texas Medical Branch. After James Thompson died, in Galveston, on April 9th 1927, he was buried in The Rest Haven Cemetery, Indiana.

Donald Hugh Thompson, founder of the Alert Bay Air Services (ABAS) in British Colombia, Canada.

DONALD HUGH THOMPSON (1920 - 2015) was the son of Alan Kinsey and Gertrude (née Thompson) and grandson of Henry Ingram Thompson (page 86). He grew up at Croft Cottage, Weaverham Road (now Croft House, page 74). In his obituary, The Times Colonist newspaper describes Donald Thompson as "...a coastal aviation pioneer..." and "...the founder of the Alert Bay Air Services...". The ABAS operate in Canada, on North Island and the British Columbia Coast. At its peak the company had over 15 planes and forty employees, at four bases, making it the largest operator of its kind in Canada. The Alert Bay Air Services was unique in that it trained its own pilots in the lore of coastal flying. Around ninety young airmen started their career with the Services and Donald Thompson, who was a much loved and respected instructor, launched the careers of many aviators.

After his studies, at Shrewsbury School, Donald worked at the Lion Salt Works, the family business in Northwich. With the onset of World War 2, he joined the RAF, at the age of twenty, and saw action in the Pacific theatre as a captain of a B-24 Liberator. He remained in touch with his entire crew for the rest of his life. It was on a trip to Winnipeg, in 1943, for flight training, that he met Jeannie Marie, his future wife. Twins, Michael and Penny, were born in 1947 and, after 18 months in England, the family moved to Canada where his second son, Jim, was born in 1957.

Donald finally stopped flying in 1968 and the last thirty years of his life were spent in Campbell River and Black Creek with his wife, Jeannie. He communicated with people around the world with beautifully, handwritten letters. In 1979, 130 of the ABAS's old pilots put on a party for the couple. Donald Hugh Thompson's death occurred on April 11th 2015, in St Joseph's Hospital, Cosmox. He was pre-deceased by Henry, his younger brother, who died in 2013; his wife, who passed away in 2008; and son, Donald Michael Thompson (2002).

ABAS, British Colombia, Canada, in 1952, founded by Donald Thompson. The planes were called "Sea Bees".

JOSEPH TRICKETT

1821 - 1903

It is likely that many Cuddington and Sandiway residents, researching the history of their property, will find that the land on which their home stands was once owned by Joseph Trickett. The Council Estate and the Wimpey, Locke and Green Field Way estates were all built on his farmland. Throughout the eighteenth and nineteenth centuries the two villages were agricultural communities. Slater's Directory for 1883 lists 25 farms in the area. One of the largest, with 220 acres, was that of Joseph Trickett.

The marriage certificate of Joseph Trickett and Mary Yearsley Warburton.

Joseph's grandfather arrived in Sandiway, in 1772, having purchased Ashbank Farm on Weaverham Road. The family went on to acquire additional dwellings and farmland, principally in Sandiway. The 1851 Census finds Joseph Trickett's unmarried Uncle, also Joseph Trickett (72 years), and the owner/occupier, living with his brother William's family at Ashbank House, a substantial detached residence neighbouring the farm. William's eldest son was Joseph Trickett and he inherited Ashbank House. Joseph and his wife, Mary Yearsley Warburton, brought up four children there: Joseph John, William, Helen and (Sarah) Annie. When he died, in 1903, Joseph left his eldest son, Joseph John, £25,805 (nearly £3m). It was he who built Cartlidge, on Norley Road. The last of the Trickett direct male line was Joseph's second son, William, who bequeathed his estate equally between his sisters, Annie and Helen. St John's Church Hall was built on land donated by Annie Trickett.

In 1948, the Ashbank Estate (said to yield a gross income of £700 per annum) passed to a distant relative on condition that he added Trickett to his name. This made him William Marsden Elverston-Trickett and it was he who finally instigated the sale of the estate: 143.5 acres, three small dairy farms, two country residences (Ashbank House and Cartlidge), three smallholdings, a semi-detached villa, eight cottages and several building plots. It is indicative of the wealth the earlier Trickett gentlemen farmers had amassed when, in 1938, Annie, the last of Joseph Trickett's children to die, left £70.147 (nearly £4.5m).

This photograph, of Ashbank House, was taken by the present owner, Mike Lloyd. Mike and his wife, Jo, have lived here for about twenty years with their children: Tom, Jessica, and twins, Catherine and Hannah. Mike is a highly successful engineer. In 2002 he joined Rolls Royce in Derby, where he was responsible for the design and supply of aerospace engine components, by 13,500 employees, at sites across six countries. Mike retired, in 2010, following completion of a £450m modernisation programme of Rolls Royce's manufacturing facilities and organisation structure.

THOMAS TAYLOR WALTON

1886 - 1951

Thomas Taylor Walton lived at Forest Hey, Sandiway. He was the co-founder of Smith and Walton Ltd., Haltwhistle, Northumberland. The firm was particularly famous for its "Hadrian" and "Centurion" paints and by the 1950's was one of the major paint companies in the country, with a staff of over 300 and factories in South Africa and

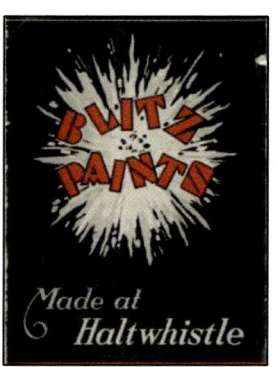

Australia. It was effectively the first to introduce emulsion paint - "Synflat" - which replaced distemper and one of the earliest to produce "Alkyd" paints, variations of which are still used today. A specialised resin plant manufactured a unique product which was used to coat the inside of batteries by Ever Ready.

During WW2 the factory developed several inventive paints which played a significant role in the war effort. They created products such as: anti glint paint to prevent reflection from glass; fire resistant paint - "Kilfyre", for rafters, to limit the destruction caused by incendiary bombs; blackout paint for windows; white kerb and road markings paint to improve safety during the blackout; "Superfine" varnish to prevent bomb shattered glass from flying; and a range of camouflage paint.

Perhaps the most ingenious of all was the "Hadrian" reflex paint - a brilliant system for factories. Light bulbs were painted orange and windows blue. During the day light could enter, but at night the orange light was filtered out by the blue of the window, providing a complete back out.

Forest Hey today, divided into two homes.

Thomas Walton agreed to sell some of his land in Sandiway for a small housing development, on condition it took the name "Hadrian" after his firm's top brand of paint. This is how Hadrian Way, as we know it today, came to be named. Thomas and his wife, known as "Pampi", had two sons, Harrison and Ronald, to whom Thomas left £68,567 (£2.1m) when he died. Smith and Walton Ltd., eventually became Crown Paints.

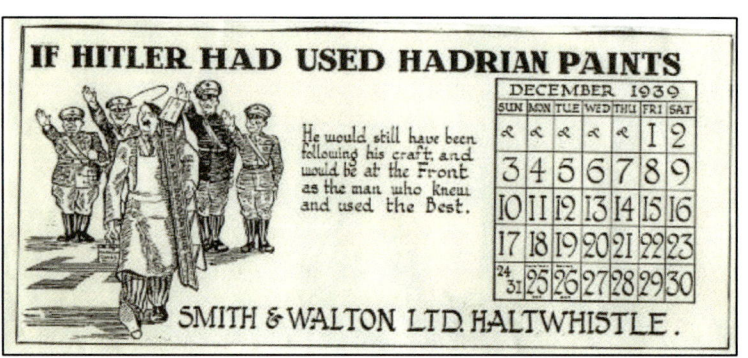

This page shows a selection of the many adverts produced by Smith and Walton during WW2.

COMMODORE FREDERICK "FRED" G. WATTS

1903 - 1989

Fred Watts and his wife with their young family.

Cdr. Frederick G. Watts is renowned for his skills as the captain of the two majestic Cunard White Star liners, *RMS Queen Elizabeth* and *RMS Queen Mary*. His parents, Christopher and Lillian Watts, were publicans in charge of the White Barn, Cuddington (page 51), and Fred lived there, as a young boy, with his brothers and sister: Charles, Christopher, Annie and Henry. He is particularly remembered for docking the "Elizabeth" in New York harbour, without the help of tugboats because the towboat men were on strike. This is an account of the event taken from a newspaper in 1964 when Fred was 61:

"The masters of two of the world's best known passenger liners met a supreme test of seamanship yesterday morning and brought their vessels into narrow slips on the Hudson River under hazardous conditions without tugs and causing little more than a scratch. The ships were the 83,673 ton Cunarder Queen Elizabeth, the world's largest passenger ship, and the 29,191 ton Cristoforo Colombo... For the Queen Elizabeth it was the first time in her 24 year-long career that she was docked unaided anywhere in the world. A harbour-wide strike forced the masters of both vessels to pit their skills against the river's currents and 35-mile-an-hour gusts of northwest winds that lashed against the long and high superstructures of the liners... it involved the safety of 14,955 passengers... The 1,031-foot Queen Elizabeth (longer than three football fields and worth $62 million at replacement cost) was pivoted around the corner of Pier 90 into the 400-foot-wide slip between that pier and Pier 92 at West 53d Street. The technique is known along the waterfront as bending a ship around the knuckle... . The Elizabeth bent her jack staff and "lost a dollar's worth of paint," Commodore Watts said. Damage to Pier 92 was estimated at $500. At 10:16 A.M. one deep throated blast of her whistle announced that she was safely alongside and that the first gangway connected her to shore. A tired but obviously pleased master said in an interview after docking, "I enjoyed it today, I suppose it was a challenge...". Cdr. Watts had said earlier that it usually took four or five tugs to berth his vessel in the same time."

Skipper, Cdr. Fred Watts, went on to complete the hazardous manoeuvres another three times before the end of that month. In 1962 he had a similar exercise whilst in command of the *Queen Mary*. During WWI Cdr. Watts served in the Royal Navy earning decorations at Dunkirk; on the island of Crete, in Greece; and off the coast of Norway, as captain of *HMS Minna*, a converted fisheries protection vessel, assigned to land Allied agents on enemy held shores. He lived, with his family, in Southampton, and died in Switzerland.

Christopher and Lillian Watts were publicans at the White Barn, in the early 1900s.

MIKE WEEDALL

b. 1956

Mike Weedall

Mike Weedall lives at The Mount, Cuddington Lane, Cuddington and was an accomplished international cross country, fell and track runner. He has represented Great Britain, England, Wales, North Wales and Cheshire. He first competed for England, in 1983, and twenty years later, in 2003, ran again for his country, at the World Fell Running Championships in the Black Forest, Germany, with a very tough six mile course. At 47 he was delighted with his 11th position. Mike had been automatically selected for the event at the preliminary trials, in Keswick, where he won the Over 45s category.

Mike Weedall has been a member of Winsford, Vale Royal, Wrexham and Pennine Fellrunners, Athletic Clubs. His original inspiration was watching the first London Marathon after which he went on to compete in marathons in London, Manchester, Bolton, Wolverhampton and Dublin with a best time of 2 hours 30 minutes. It is in no small part due to his enthusiasm and dedication to these three disciplines that the Vale Royal Athletic Club has produced 24 full internationals since it's opening in 1994.

Mike Weedall - no. 130 - in the 2007 Tattenhall Tough Teams Challenge.

There are many highlights to Mike's career. In 1998 he won the Sandstone Trail 16 mile race by over five minutes, breaking a long standing Over Forties course record and in 1999 he competed for Great Britain at the World Masters Championships, in the 10,000m Cross Country and the 5,000m track event, held in Gateshead.

In 2006, Mike entered the British Masters Athletic Federation Championships, Birmingham, where he won a gold medal in both the half marathon and 10,000m track and silver in the 5,000m. In the same year he won silver at the British Irish Masters Cross Country held in Falkirk and represented Great Britain at the Masters in Belgium over 5,000m on the track. This is the biggest event in the world for the Over 40s and athletes have to be selected as they are running for their country. In 2007 Mike crossed the line in 1st place in the British and Irish Masters Cross Country Championships, Belfast, and won a bronze medal at the BMAF Road Relays in Birmingham, running the 3rd fastest leg of the day. In 2013 Mike led his Wrexham team, of four, home to win the British 10K final at Portsmouth. For team mate, Bernie Jones, it was his fifteenth British Championship medal. Bernie, another successful runner, also lives in the village, in Sandington Drive.

A former chef and Middlewich postman, who lived in Winsford, and then Rudheath, before moving to Cuddington, Mike Weedall has not run competitively since 2013.

The Mount, Cuddington Lane.

GEORGE WILBRAHAM

1741 - 1813

George Wilbraham, the founder of Delamere Lodge, by Battoni, about 1764 - 65.

George Wilbraham's combined wealth, vision and illustrious ancestry, make him the most important gentleman to ever grace the village of Cuddington. In 1784, George left his family seat, Townsend House, Nantwich, and built Delamere Lodge on the land which is now Delamere Park. His arrival impacted upon the lives of everyone for miles around, bringing improved farming methods, cottages to house an army of estate and domestic workers and a veritable array of employment opportunities. It is believed that George Wilbraham favoured Cuddington because it was in the midst of excellent hunting country and close to Tarporley, where he was a founder member of the Tarporley Hunt Club.

George engaged the radical architect, Samuel Wyatt, to design and build his new home. Whilst this was underway he lived at Hefferston Grange, Weaverham (page 119), with his wife, Maria Harvey, and their young family. Six of their offspring were born at Hefferston: Maria, Emma, Roger, George, William and Elizabeth, and Louisa and Anna at Delamere Lodge. Wyatt's other enterprises included Trinity House in London and the Longships, Dungeness and Flamborough Head lighthouses. In Cheshire, he constructed Bostock Hall, Hooton Hall and Doddington Hall and redesigned the mansion at Tatton.

Delamere House about a century ago, a development of Wyatt's Delamere Lodge. The principal part of the Lodge was constructed of Exmoor granite and photos of Doddington Hall and Coton House, Warwickshire, probably best reflect the appearance of the original dwelling. It was by far the most impressive residence in the district.

Once established in Wyatt's mansion, George set his mind to the cultivation of the large open fields on his estate which amounted to several thousand acres. He introduced horse powered machinery, crop rotation, shippons with concrete floors, separate stalls for calving and Dutch barns for storing hay. The 36 tenement workers on his land became tied workers on the estate rather than exercising their feudal rights on common land, as before. George Wilbraham's model farming techniques attracted interest from far and wide. Although clearly a busy man, George found time to be a Member of Parliament for Bodmin, Cornwall (1889 - 90), the Sheriff of Cheshire and a local magistrate.

George Wilbraham was also one of the instigators of the Tarporley Races, which thrived until well into the twentieth Century. In 1776, the Tarporley Hunt Club held a sweepstake at

Crabtree Green, on the Wilbraham Estate, with seven runners. The Green had been used as a racecourse since the mid-17th century. Now the contest became an annual event and, by 1809, a permanent fixture in the Racing Calendar. After the enclosure of Delamere Forest in 1812, the races moved first to Billington's Training Ground, Delamere, near The Fishpool Inn, and then to Cotebrook, on a course by the modern A49, rented from Lord Shrewsbury. In 1875, the race meeting, by then held in April and known as the "Tarporley Hunt Steeplechase", moved to Saighton Farm on the Duke of Westminster's Estate. Its location moved, one last time, in 1877, to the Arderne Estate on the outskirts of Tarporley, where a permanent course was later constructed. The event became increasingly popular with spectators in the late 19th and early 20th century and they arrived by a special train. The members' rode their race in hunting costume. In 1926, the club formed a limited company, "Tarporley Steeplechases", to run the meetings. The event attracted 10,000 spectators in 1937, but the races stopped after 1939, due to WWI, and never resumed; "Tarporley Steeplechases'" was wound up in 1963.

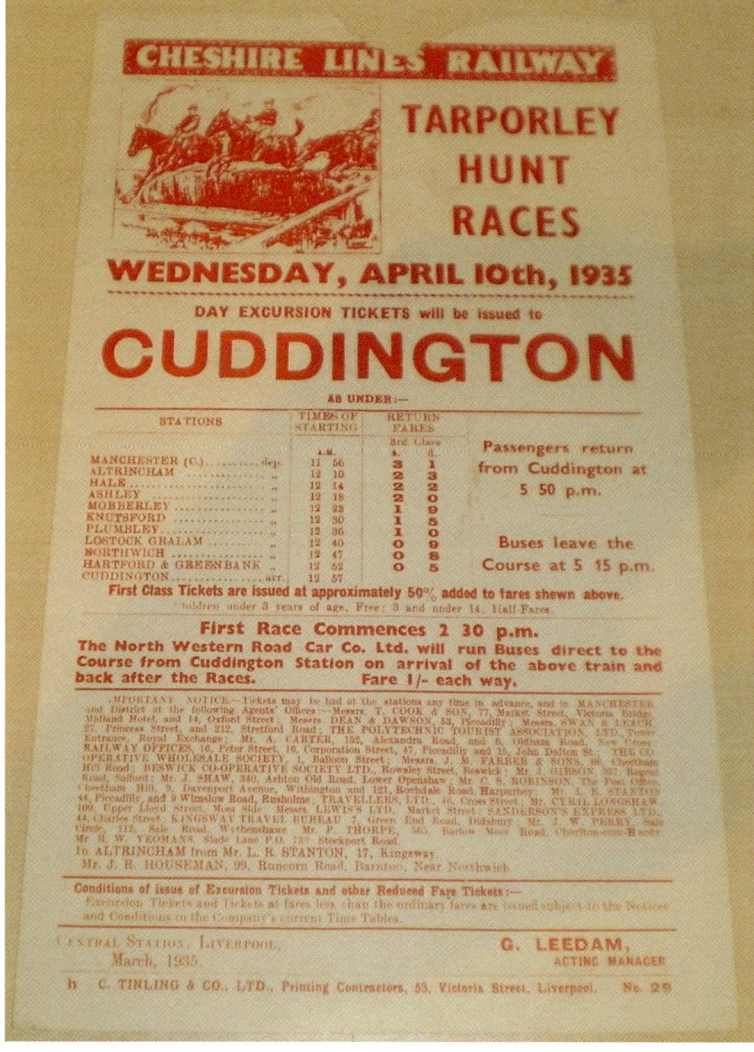

A Cheshire Lines Railway poster from the 1930s, advertising the special train they would be providing for those wishing to have a day out at the Tarporley Races, an event instigated, in no small part, by George Wilbraham over 150 years before.

George Wilbraham's death occurred at Delamere Lodge on December 3rd 1813 and his remains were interred in the family vault in Nantwich Church although, whilst living in Cuddington, George worshipped at Weaverham where there are still old Georgian box seats used by his family in the Wilbraham Chapel. Daniel Lysons, a notable English antiquary and topographer of the time, wrote of George Wilbraham at the time of his death:

"...few men have passed through this life with a more unsullied reputation. He was of a modest and unambitious nature and, though well versed in his earlier years in those languages and studies which form an accomplished gentleman, he chose rather, as he advanced in age, to addict himself to those pursuits which are practically useful to mankind, so that he could leave behind him the reputation of an enlightened agriculturist, a kind landlord and master with an affectionate and respected parent."

After George's demise, a succession of Wilbraham heirs adapted and added to the contents of the House and Estate. They established an extensive library and covered the walls with rare works of art. There were many portraits including a Rembrandt, a Salvador Rosa and *Portrait of a Lady* by Titian. On their vast estate, Cuddington Hall Farm, Poplar Farm, Barratwitch (or Barrastitch), Cuddington Bank Cottages and The Mount - all on Cuddington Lane; and Water Mill Farm, off Norley Road, were all properties built by the Wilbraham family, and there were others further afield. However, by the 1930s, the house was in a state of disrepair under the last incumbent, George Hugh de Vernon. His new wife, Mary Roberta "Bertha" Bullock, disliked the place, so they built a new home, Delamere Manor (page 5), overlooking Cuddington Pool. The contents of Delamere House were sold off in a three day sale and then George Hugh de Vernon Wilbraham set about systematically selling the fabric of the house until only the foundations were left.

Portrait of a Lady by Titian, 97.8 x 74cm. Now at the National Gallery of Art, Washington D.C. Its value is said to be immeasurable.

For those interested to know the full story of the Wilbraham's and Delamere Park they can do no better than refer to *The Story of Delamere House and Delamere Park* by A. D. Coxhead and R. M. Bevan.

WORLD WAR DEAD

There is no one more worthy of note than the servicemen, from Cuddington and Sandiway, who gave their lives for their country in the First and Second World Wars. They are as follows:-

WW1 (1914 - 1918)

Pte. Henry S. Barlow (42y)

Bdr. Joseph Barnes (32y)

Pte. Joseph Bell (21y)

Pte. Walter Bell (28y)

Pte. John Birtwistle (25y)

Pte. William Birtwistle (19y)

Pte. Albert Christopher (27y)

Pte. Frederick J. Christopher (21y)

Pte. William J. Deamer (23y)

Lt. George Dewhurst (24y)

Pte. Fred Fowles (26y)

Cpl. Arthur Gerrard (31y)

Pte. John J. Gerrard (27y)

Pte. James Kettle (29y)

L. Cpl. A. Sydney Newall (25y)

Pte. John Nield (31y)

Lt. Arthur Palfreyman (32y)

Pte Edward Tomkinson (33y)

Pte. Dennis Wakefield (21y)

Pte. George Wakefield (24y)

Pte. Thomas E. Price (22y)

Pte. Ralph Ramsden (23y)

WW2 (1939 - 1945)

Flt. Sgt. Leonard C. Barker (22y)

Lt. Frederick Burgess (24y)

Cpl. Robert Conkie (30y)

Sgt. Harry Poole (27y)

Pte. Malcolm Roberts (19y)

Lt. Thomas Rowland DFC (32y)

Sgt. Michael Stilliard (19y)

Flt. Lt. Ralph Eric Tallis DFC (21y)

Gnr. Douglas K. Thompson (34y)

Gdsn. William S. Roberts (28y)

May they rest in Peace

JACQUELINE YALLOP

b. 1969

Jacqueline Yallop as she appears on her website.

Jacqueline Yallop is an author, a senior lecturer of creative writing at the University of Aberystwyth and a master class leader for The Guardian newspaper and The Faber Academy. Her mentoring service, The Writers Wheel, offers courses for budding authors. With her parents, Joe and Christine Yallop, Jacqueline moved from Solihull, West Midlands, to Moorlands Avenue, Cuddington, in 1985, and lived there until her marriage in 1994. She now divides her time between the United Kingdom and South-West France.

Jacqueline Yallop studied English Literature at Lincoln College, Oxford, before becoming a museum curator. She worked with a variety of collections including that of the Wordsworth Trust archive at Dove Cottage in the Lake District, and the Ruskin collection in Sheffield. In 2006, Jacqueline completed a PhD at the University of Sheffield, exploring some of the links between literature, objects, collecting and museums in the nineteenth century.

Since 2009 Jacqueline has published five books, three fiction and two non-fiction which are shown below. All have received excellent reviews:

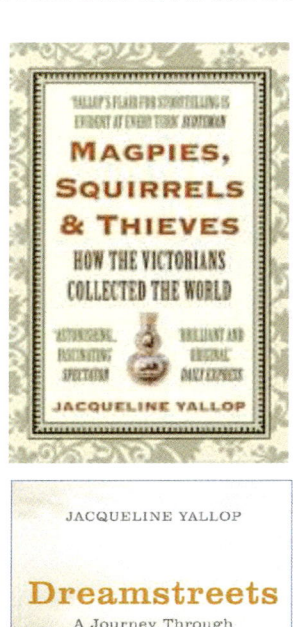
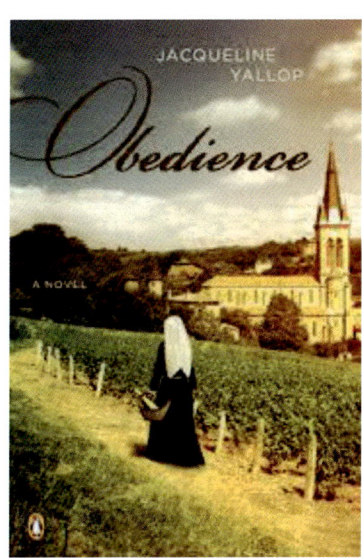
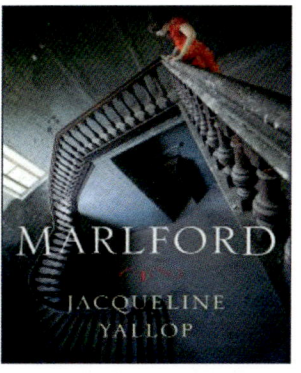
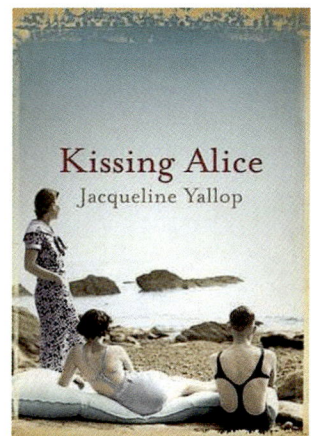

RICHARD JOSEPH YEOWARD "THE BANANA KING"

1865 - 1937

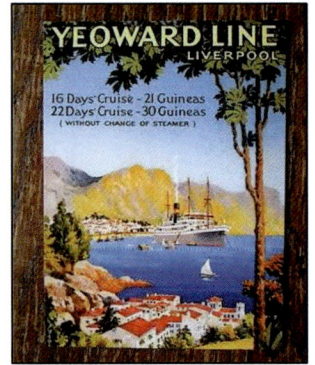

Yeoward Line posters advertising their "Banana Cruises".

In the early twentieth century, until his death, Richard Yeoward resided at White Lodge, Norley Road (page 59). The property then comprised The Lodge, The Mews and the adjacent field (now Cuddington and Sandiway Playing Field). Mr Yeoward was known by the locals as "The Banana King" as he and his brother owned extensive banana plantations in Tenerife and introduced the first passenger cruises to the island aboard the steamships with which they imported bananas back to the UK.

The progress of the company was phenomenal. Richard and his brother, Louis Herbert Yeoward (1867-1916) formed "Yeoward Brothers" in 1894, at 24, James Street, Liverpool, and in 1924 it became the Yeoward Line Ltd. It operated fruit, vegetable, and passenger ships, from Liverpool to Spain, Portugal and The Canary Islands. This continued until 1954 when the last boat was scrapped, although the company continued the fruit trade using the Spanish Aznar Line as carriers. The firm developed the study of the comfort of their patrons to a fine art and prided themselves on the standard of accommodation and service offered on their "Banana Boat Cruises".

As Richard and Louis grew older the "Yeoward Line" was taken over by Richard's two sons, Raymond (born 1897) and Bernard (1905); for a time, Bernard and his sister, Evaline, lived at White Lodge. Bernard was a man of many interests. In 1927, he was twice a winner at Crufts with his Golden Retriever, Stanthorne Serenus, and he played exhibition tennis matches in France with Jean Borota - famed as "The Bouncing Basque from Biarritz" - a twice singles, and three times doubles, winner at Wimbledon, as well as taking the French, Australian and US titles. Bernard married Eileen Lorna Terry and retired from the firm, at the end of 1930, leaving Raymond in charge. Evaline married Reginald Howarth, the grandson of the inventor of Elastoplast, who also lived in the village.

In Liverpool, the Yeoward Line's success is seen as an excellent example of enterprise in the early twentieth century, whilst, in Tenerife, there are many reminders of the "line". The British School, Taoro Park, Peurto de la Cruz (opened in 1968) was originally named the Yeoward School; a street in

Richard Yeoward (1936-2015) was the son of Bernard Yeoward and the grandson of R. J. Yeoward. He was an Olympic bobsleigh and skiing competitor and a first class yachtsman.

the Botanico area of the same town is called Avenida Richard Yeoward, in honour of the entrepreneur; and a large section of the land and cliffs above Puerto de la Cruz is officially called The Costa Yeoward. A direct descendent of Richard, Tony Yeoward, still lives on the island. When he died, Richard Joseph Yeoward was buried in Whitegate cemetery. His wife, Bertha Elizabeth Evans lived on at White Lodge for several years, before passing away at Rhosneigr, Anglesey, in 1958. Her effects amounted to £68,000 (£1.5m).

-Above are three "Yeoward Line" steamships from the 1910s to the 1930s: the Aguila, the Aloudiz and the Avocet.

Below are pictured playing cards from a "Yeoward Line" cruise ship.

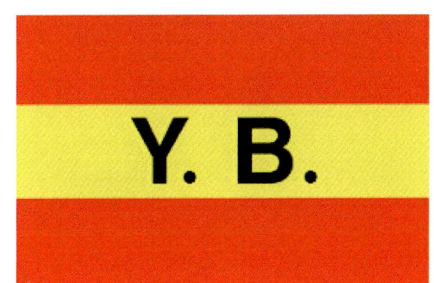

ANNIE MARSHALL YOUNG

1887 - 1984

Annie Marshall Young
Photo: Mark Bevan Collection

There will be few older village residents who have not heard the name, Annie Young. She was a dedicated ward sister in several hospitals, a lecturer on nursing throughout Cheshire, a tireless community worker for sixty years and the mother of Dr Percy Marshall Young, an eminent musicologist. After the death of her husband, William Joseph Young, who was twice Mayor of Northwich, Annie commenced her retirement in Cockpit Lane, Sandiway and then Forest Close, Cuddington.

Born in Kent, she moved to 12, David Street, Northwich, before the Second World War to work as a nurse at Victoria Infirmary. During WWI Annie was "Sister in Charge" of the British Red Cross, Ley Convalescent Home for wounded soldiers in Winnington and, afterwards, was involved at the Welfare Centre opposite Northwich Infirmary. During WW2 she trained and lectured as an Air Raid Precautions instructor and worked as a nursing sister at Runcorn Cottage Hospital. Among her many offices, she was chairman of Northwich Rural District Council, as a Conservative councillor, from 1955-1974.

Dr Percy Young

Annie Young's son, Percy Young, had three passions: music, education and football (he was a dedicated fan of Wolverhampton Wanderers Football team). His career and sixty plus publications reflect this. In 1930 he won an organ scholarship to Selwyn College, Cambridge, and after graduating completed a doctorate at Trinity College, Dublin. From 1934-1937 he was a Director of Music at Stranmillis Teacher Training College, Belfast, and from 1937-1944, a Musical Adviser to Stoke-on-Trent L.E.A. He became Director of Music at Wolverhampton College of Technology in 1944, a position he held until 1966. Percy Young did many engaging musical talks on BBC radio, for all ages, and was an Honorary Fellow of Selwyn College, Cambridge, from 1998 until his death. He wrote over fifty music books, some general, but also biographies of composers such as Handel, Vaughan Williams, Mozart and Debussy.

His most devoted study was to Edward Elgar. After Elgar's death, his daughter, Clarice, gave Dr Young Sir Edward's magnificent white and gilt Schiedmayer piano, which was housed at Annie's home in Sandiway. He owned many items of Elgar memorabilia, including paintings and Elgar's shaving mirror! Young was as prolific a composer as an author but he was best known for his reconstruction of Elgar's only opera, *The Spanish Lady*, which Elgar left unfinished when he died in 1934. After the death of Percy's first wife, Netta, with whom he had three sons and a daughter, he married Renée Morris, who survived him when he died in 2004.

This Blue Plaque now hangs on the outside of Percy Young's old home in Wolverhampton. Left - Percy as a young man.

MORE MILLIONAIRES

OTTIWELL FRANK WATERFIELD (1865 - 1943) was a cotton merchant who owned businesses in Egypt, Paris and Manchester, where he was in partnership with Henry Platford and Robert Garside. In the early 1900s, Ottiwell was living at Cuddington Grange (page 105) with his wife, Constance Manners-Sutton, who was born in Sialkot, India. They travelled extensively and, in 1913, sailed from Liverpool to New York on the legendary ship, Mauritania. Ottiwell Waterfield was born in Richmond, Surrey, the son of an Eton school master who was later appointed Principal of Temple Grove School, East Sheen. Ottiwell went up to Trinity College, Cambridge, where he gained a BA, and finally passed away, childless, in Kensington, leaving £22,396 (nearly £1m).

The Mauritania in 1907.

CHARLES ARTHUR REISS (1874 - 1949) lived at Sandiway Manor, Norley Road (page 52), in the early 1900s. He was a cotton merchant with the East India Company at 126, The Royal Exchange, Manchester, but his company, Reiss Brothers, also had offices in Mincing Lane, London, and Orleans House, Liverpool. Charles Reiss was a Liberal Unionist and a keen charity worker, founding a boys' orphanage in Blackheath. Born in Swinton, Lancashire, and educated at Harrow and Balliol College, Oxford, on 15th June 1882, Charles married Florence Lacy Baggallay, the daughter of Sir Richard Baggallay, who was a Conservative MP and Attorney General under Disraeli. Charles and Florence had four children who were baptised: Richard Leopold (1883), Horace Baggallay (1886), Stephen Lacy (1889) and Caroline Sylvia (1893). As chairman of the "Garden Cities and Town Planning Association of Great Britain", Richard was the founder of Welwyn Garden City. Stephen was killed in action in 1915. When Charles Reiss and his wife had Sandiway Manor, it was said to be one of the focal points for social life in Cheshire.

Richard Leopold Reiss, the founder of Welwyn Garden City.

DONALD BEITH (1878 - 1947) was another cotton merchant and lived at Gorstage Hall (page 5) in the early to mid-twentieth century. He was Governing Director of his family's firm, Beith, Stevenson & Co., of Manchester and Glasgow; Deputy Chairman of D. Anderson and Son, of London, Belfast and Manchester; Chairman of Cheshire Public House Trust Co. and director of the London and Lancashire insurance Co. Donald also gained directorships of the Manchester and County Bank, the Royal Exchange and the Ship Canal Company, and was on the board of numerous medical institutions. He travelled widely, to Canada, Seattle in the US, and Yokohama in Japan. In 1903, Donald married Florence and there followed five children: Alexander, Evelyn, Donald, Norris and Julia. Although born in Withington, Manchester, Donald Beith's family was originally from Scotland and it was to Dumfriesshire that he retired and found his final resting place. It is known that he died a wealthy man but his effects were sealed.

Around 1870, yet another cotton merchant and broker, **WILLIAM MARRIOTT** (1833 - 1893), lived at Forest Hill House, Sandiway. He was born and carried out his business in Liverpool under the name of Marriott and Co., with his partners, George Arthur Holt, George Irvine Washington and William F. Leather. Both William and his father, Joseph Marriott, were held in high esteem by the Cotton Brokers of Liverpool. When William Marriott died he left £16,976 (over £1.5m).

The east wing of Forest Hill House today; little changed from the nineteenth century.

GEORGE REYNOLDS DAVIES (1842 - 1918) lived in the locality for some years, but it wasn't until 1885, after his marriage to Katherine, in Kensington, that he came to live in Sandiway, at Forest Hill House. A direct descendent of Edward III, in 1881 Mr Davies was resident at Agden Hall, Altrincham, describing himself as a "cotton and shipping merchant". His main offices were at 101, Portland Street, Manchester, under the name George Frazer and Co. The son of David Reynolds Davies of Mere Old Hall, as a youngster at Harrow, George Davies represented his school, and later Cheshire, at cricket. He was a JP for Knutsford and Cheshire and was succeeded by his sons, John and George, to whom he bequeathed £62,588 (nearly £4m).

CAPTAIN EDWARD LEE TOWNSHEND (1868 - 1914) lived at Gorstage Hall (page 2) for the first two decades of the nineteenth century but was born at Wincham Hall, Northwich. The family estate sat on top of some of Cheshire's richest salt deposits which were to be a significant source of income for the family. Captain Townshend owned at least three prosperous salt mines in Wincham. He moved first to Delamere Cottage, now Sandiway Manor (page 52), and then to Gorstage

Wincham Hall in about 1900, the birthplace of Edward Lee Townshend.

Hall to raise his children with his wife, Mildred, the youngest daughter of Colonel Cholmondeley. It is said that Captain Townshend quarrelled with all he met. One Christmas, those invited to dinner were shown into the dining room, only to be met with no food and two prowling bears. The guests fled through the windows! Nevertheless, The Townshend's Arms in Wincham and Townshend Road in Lostock were both named after him. The former fell over 70 years ago due to subsidence. Captain Edward Lee Townshend left the vast sum of £84,447 (£8.7m).

GEORGE FREDERICK GEE (1873 - 1945) lived at Abbotsford (page 83) with his wife, Ellen, and describes himself as a "draper and clothier" in Manchester. He passed way in 1945 leaving

£60,777 (£2.4m) to his sons, "John Frederick Gee and George Neville Gee, company directors and Charles Reginald Gee, engineer". George Gee was an accomplished field naturalist and was elected a fellow of the Royal Entomological Society of London in 1923. In 1940, a rare specimen of a Great Skua was presented to Chester Museum by "G.F. Gee of Abbotsford, Cuddington".

Another Abbotsford resident was **JAMES CLEGHORNE** (1841 - 1920). He was an engineer who part owned the Leftwich iron foundry, Cleghorne, Bates & Co. or Cleghorne and Wilkinson, as it was to become. Pumping gear made by the firm has been found in Middlewich, and at Port Dinorwic Harbour quayside, where the bollards, and lock sluice operating equipment, are marked "Cleghorne and Wilkinson Engineers, Northwich", and date from 1901/1902. James also built 14 houses for his workers in Jubilee Street, Northwich. Foundries were hazardous places, and in 1893 a number of men were engaged in lowering heavy casting, when the chain by which it was suspended snapped. Oswald Yearsley, a furnace man of 21 years, was struck in the chest by falling metal and died instantly. This would have been a difficult day for Mr Cleghorne but James and his wife, Whillamina, knew sadness even closer to home. Two of their three sons were to die young: John in 1885 when he was 18, and William in 1895 at the age of 21. The family are buried at St Wilfred's, Northwich. On his death, James was able to leave £51,953 (£2.4m) to his remaining son, also James.

The Homestead, now Redwalls, designed by John Douglas for B. J. Sanby.

BERNARD J. SANBY (1859 - 1936) left £39,000 (£2.4m) and for thirty years was resident at The Homestead, now Redwalls, on Weaverham Road. It is a Grade II listed building. In 1906/7 the large detached house and stables were designed and built, for Mr Sanby, by John Douglas (page 26) who also sold him the land. As a young man, Bernard Sanby worked for his father as an "auction collector", travelling the roads and lanes around Manchester picking up works of art to take back to his father's sale rooms, which eventually became his own.

OLIVER ASHWORTH (1882 - 1944) resided at Gorstage Hall (page 5) in the 1890s and accumulated the massive amount of £331,975 (£13.5m) as the co-owner, with his brothers, James and George, of a carpet making factory in Lancashire. The firm, Bridge End Felt and Carpet Works, Waterfoot, Lancs, was founded by his father, Richard Ashworth, who bequeathed the massive sum of £267,283 (£15m) to his sons in 1928. Oliver Ashworth was born in Hillingdon, Lancashire, and died at Durran, a property in Rawstenstall, designed and built for him in circa 1907 at a cost of £5,000 (£0.5m). His son, Melville Oliver Ashworth, was a distinguished soldier, serving as a major in Gallipoli in the 6th Battalion of the British Army.

Durran, an arts and crafts house built for Oliver Ashworth, at a cost of £5,000, in 1907.

WILLIAM LAWRENCE TURNER (1884 - 1950) lived at Sandiway Manor (page 52) in the 1940s. He was a metallurgist, involved in the manufacture of stainless steel, particularly high speed, tool steel; an alloy which was quicker and cheaper to produce. His father, also William Turner, who founded the family's Sheffield based firm, had at least three patents to his name, dating from 1918/19, and was held in high regard within his profession. William Turner Jr married Sybil Kiernan, the eldest daughter of A. J. Thompson (page 87), and widow of J. F. Kiernan of Woodbank, Chester Road, Sandiway. Mr Kiernan, who passed away in 1912, left £11,311 (£1.2m), to his son, "Alfred Thomas Bernard Kiernan, W. L. Turner, metallurgist, and Florence Percival". William Turner's effects amounted to £35,258 (£1.1m).

An advert from 1891, when William Turner's father was in charge of William Turner and Son.

CECIL BERNARD MORGAN (1874 - 1942) lived at Blakemere (page 50). On his death he left nearly a million pounds to his son, Vernon Eversfield Morgan, who represented Great Britain at the 1928 Olympics (1904-1992). Cecil Morgan made his money in the textile industry and was a member of the Cloth Worker's Company, an ancient Livery Company, in London. He was appointed their Master for the year 1939/40, a job which mainly involved representing the Company on ceremonial occasions. Cecil Morgan went on to gain the freedom of the City of London. When Blakemere Hall and its house contents were sold in 1938, many treasures were listed: eighteenth century English furniture; antique mahogany grandfather clocks and a Queen Anne parquetry grandmother clock; an important collection of Ralph Wood pottery; Chinese porcelain; weapons, and silver by Paul de Lamerie and other well known makers. The Cloth Workers Company hold two valuable pieces of silver once belonging to Cecil Bernard Morgan - a drinking horn and a gavel with an ivory handle.

Between 1911 and 1918, **ARTHUR ERNEST LAWLEY** (1875 - 1920), and his wife, Elizabeth, lived in lavish style at Forest Hey, Sandiway (page 90), with their daughters, Joyce and Francis. Arthur Lawley was a cotton merchant and a partner in the firm Lawley Everett and Co., Ancoats, Manchester. In 1918 he purchased Hilston House and the Glanmonnow Estate, 3,800 acres in all: both are near Hereford. He was to die only two years later, having accumulated the substantial sum of £368,716 (£17.1m).

Hilston House

RICHARD "DICKIE" HARDING (1783 - 1880). Morris and Co.'s Directory, 1874, lists amongst Cuddington's "gentry", a certain Richard Harding, living at "Robin Hood". The 1836-51 Cheshire Tithe Maps show an eight acre plot, divided into three field strips and named "Robin Hood's Butts". It is on Norley Road, where Cuddington Grange stands today. As this stretch of road was named by locals "Dickie Harding's Hill", well into the twentieth century, it seems likely that this is where Richard Harding lived. Whether "Dickie", A. E. Lloyd or the third owner, Henry I. Thompson (page 86), renamed the house Cuddington Grange, is uncertain. Born in Church Coppenhall, but living in Cuddington by the time of the 1951 census, Dickie Harding was buried in St Mary's Churchyard, Weaverham. His estate amounted to £12,000 (over £1m).

Above left: A drawing of Dickie Harding by George Stocks, Cuddington's station master at the time (Mark Bevan Collection). Right: Cuddington Grange in its heyday.

RICHARD C. LOWCOCK (1852 - 1922) was another whose family made their wealth on the back of cotton. In the early 1900s he resided at White Lodge, Norley Road (page 59). Born at Ollerton Grange, Knutsford, by 1871 Richard Lowcock was a manager within his father, John Lowcock's, cotton manufacturing firm. The business employed some 1,000 workers and was a guarantor for the building of the Manchester Ship Canal. Richard married Henrietta Ogden and there followed a number of children including six boys. By the time of his death, Richard Lowcock had amassed £35,313 (£1.5m).

Ollerton Grange, Knutsford.

ARTHUR TREVALYAN NEILSON (1861 - 1921) lived at Holmwood, Weaverham Road, from about 1910 until his death in 1921 when he bequeathed the large sum of £172,025 (£8.75m). Mr Neilson had been a successful stockbroker in Liverpool in the firm Neilson and Clegg. When he died an oak screen was erected at the North end of Norley Church by his sister, Sybil Harriet Neilson, in memory of her brother. Sybil had married Colonel William Lee Pilkington (from the famous Pilkington glass manufacturing family) who lived at Norley Bank, Norley. Arthur was buried in St Nicholas's church, Halewood, his childhood home.

Holmwood as it is today, little changed from the days of Arthur Neilson.

THE TARPORLEY HUNT CLUB

The Tarporley Hunt meets at the Blue Cap, Sandiway.

It would be impossible to write any History of Cuddington and Sandiway without including The Tarporley Hunt Club, founded on November 14th 1762 at The Swan Hotel, Tarporley. Whatever our feelings about the "sport" and some may be very strong, its members were, by and large, young, charismatic, skilful horsemen, with distinguished military careers, indulging in a fashionable pursuit of the day. The Hunt met regularly at The Blue Cap Hotel, Chester Road, Sandiway. Hunting was the magnet which drew "gentlemen" from all over the county, and beyond, and some made their homes in Cuddington and Sandiway.

Good friends, Lowry Egerton Cole, later the 4th Earl of Enniskillen - top, and Edmund Park Yates - bottom.
(Mark Bevan Collection)

Two of these were, good friends, **VISCOUNT LOWRY EGERTON COLE** (1845 - 1924), later the 4th Earl of Enniskillen, and **CAPTAIN EDMUND WALDERGRAVE "PUFFLES" PARK YATES** (1836 - 1896). The Earl of Enniskillen, or "Coly" as he was known, was said to be very popular "...one of the pretty, joyous young men ...of London Society. Blessed with good looks, an even temper and a determination to make the best of this world" (*Vanity Fair, "Men of the Day"* series). Although his home was in Ireland, he rented several grand houses in the district, including Pettypool (page116), Cuddington Grange (page 105), and Cassia Lodge, Whitegate. He would stay for long periods with his wife, Charlotte, children: Charlotte, Kathleen, John, Florence and Galbraith, and a staff of around 17. His third daughter, Florence, married Lord Delamere of Vale Royal Abbey (page123). Captain Park Yates, of Sandiway Lodge (page 5), was married to Emily Clementina Churchill Dixie, and his family seat was Ince Hall, Wigan. One day the two pals were out hunting and Captain Park-Yates fell badly from his horse. "Coly" sat up all night with his stricken chum hoping his life would be spared but it wasn't to be. He passed away the next morning leaving his wife well provided for with £66,782 (£6.2m). The West Window in St John's Church, Sandiway, which depicts Faith Hope and Charity, is dedicated to his memory. The memorial reads:

"To the glory of God and in remembrance of Edward Waldergrave Park Yates who endeared himself to all during the 19 years he lived in Sandiway. This window is placed here by his friends."

Jersey de Knoop, shortly before his death in 1916.

Another resident was **CAPT. JOHN JULIUS JERSEY DE KNOOP** (1876 - 1916) who sojourned at Cuddington Grange (page 105) for several years. As well as hunting, he rowed for Oxford in the annual Boat Race in 1896 and 1897 and was President of Witton Albion Football Club and the Mid-Cheshire Bowling Association. When he stood for Parliament, as the Conservative candidate for Northwich, in 1910, he only lost out by 2.8% of the vote. Born at Calveley Hall, Bunbury, Jersey de Knoop was the son of Baron de Knoop who, in Manchester, during WWI, spoke publicly, about the lack of arms for the soldiers on the front. Not mincing his words, he proclaimed, "...thousands were killed largely because of the lack of ammunition". His speech attracted a lot of attention and he was severely reprimanded by the War Office but Baron de Knoop had good reason to speak so passionately. After a successful spell in the Cheshire Yeomanry his son fought with the Camel Corps in Egypt and was killed in August 1916 whilst leading a desert foray against the Turks. Jersey left a wife, Evelyn Elizabeth Fletcher MBE, five children: Barbara, Margaret, Wilfred, Joan and John, and £172,670 (nearly £16m). His young daughters were often seen around the village, in a gig pulled by eight Shetland ponies.

Jersey de Knoop, after beating Cambridge in the Boat Race in 1897.

Lord Berkley Paget

LORD BERKLEY CHARLES SYDNEY PAGET (1844 - 1913), built Blakemere Hall (page 50) in 1878 to be near his beloved Tarporley Hunt Club. His grandfather, Henry Paget, the 1st Marquess of Anglesey, had been second in command to Wellington at the Battle of Waterloo. One of his legs needed to be amputated and Henry was fitted with the first articulated, wooden limb in the world which was used right up to the first world war. It is on display at Plas Newedd, Anglesey. On Lord Berkley's death his widow, Florence, received £22,000 (£2.25m) which she, in turn, bequeathed to her son, Richard C. Berkley Paget.

HARRY RAWSON (1818 - 1888) kept a detailed Hunting Journal from the early 1860s until his death in 1888. Gordon Fergusson's book, *The Green Collars*, an absorbing history of The Hunt, regularly quotes from Harry Rawson's manuscripts. They give a colourful picture of the many meets over the years, the accidents in the field, the weather, the eventual

Two pictures of Harry Rawson out hunting. Left - Harry Rawson and F. E. Massey Esq. about to be thrown from his horse. Right - Harry Rawson in the ditch!
Paintings by Frank Massey

appearance of a "profusion" of lady riders which led to some distractions amongst the gentlemen, but laments his own lack of a wife and how he is "plagued" by gout. A member of a family of insurance brokers from Wheathill House, Huyton, in 1881 he lived at Toolerstone Farm, Sandiway. The enormous value of his estate amounted to £90,000 (over £8m). Harry Rawson is buried in Weaverham Churchyard.

Toolerstone Farm, now Toolerstone House (page 71).

For many years Dalefords (then Dale Ford) in Dalefords Lane, Sandiway, was a hunting lodge on Lord Delamere's Vale Royal Estate and three enthusiastic Hunt members made full use of it. In 1841, millionaire, **CAPTAIN JOHN "JACK" WHITE** moved in, having just taken over the Mastership of the Cheshire Hounds. Known throughout the land as "Leicestershire White' with a reputation as one of the hardest and fastest riders of his time, and a physique, voice and whiskers to match, he once rode 250 miles in a day between breakfast and 11 p.m. He continued to occupy Dalefords until his death in 1866 when the dwelling was taken by **HENRY REGINALD "REGGIE" CORBET** (1832 - 1902) of Adderley Hall. Henry was Master of the Cheshire Hounds for 35 years and kept a fox as a pet. He was described as an "unrivalled horseman... his horses all jumped faultlessly and never refused". He was brother-in-law to Philip Grey Egerton of Oulton Park. **LIEUTENANT COMMANDER RALPH MIDWOOD** (1896 - 1970), a cotton broker and horse trainer, formerly of Rookery Hall, Worleston, and Oakmere Hall (page 122), was the last member of the Tarporley Hunt to reside at Dalefords. In WWI he was captain of the Montgomeryshire Yeomanry, and in WW2, Battalion Commander of the Cheshire Home Guard. In 1941 he was left a wealthy man when his father, Walter Midwood of Calveley Hall, near Tarporley, died, leaving him £255,797 (£12.8m).

Henry "Reggie" Corbet

Captain John White on Alice Grey.
Painting by Frank Massey.

Dale Ford, now Dalefords, a Hunting Lodge on the Vale Royal Estate.

HENRY "HARRY" BROOKE (1798 - 1884) was a member of the Tarporley Hunt Club for 63 years and their secretary for 18 of them (1847-65). He was High Sheriff of Cheshire (1948-49); Captain of the Cheshire Yeomanry in his younger days; and a keen associate of the Lancashire and Cheshire Historical Society. Harry Brooke was born at Norton Priory, Runcorn, the son of Thomas Brooke of Ashbrook Hall, Church Minshull, and the nephew of Sir Richard Brooke, the sixth Baronet of Norton. In the 1840s he was living at Forest Hill, Sandiway (page 102), but by the mid 1850s had moved to Grange Hall, Weaverham, the home of his ninety year old Aunt Mary who was the widow of Sir Richard Brooke and daughter of Lady Mary Cholmondeley (page 125). Each year Harry distributed 100 shillings amongst the needy of Church Minshull and in 1858 a new school was built there, a gift from Henry Brooke in memory of Mr C. B. Davies of Eardswick Hall, Minshull Vernon. Henry eventually inherited Ashbrook Hall where he died in 1884 leaving £21,811 (over £2m) to his family.

Henry "Harry" Brooke, from a painting by Frank Massey.

A celebrity who stayed in the village in order to ride with The Hunt was **JIMMY EDWARDS** (real name: James Keith O'Neil D. F. C., 1920 - 1988). He would stay at The Lodge belonging to Delamere Manor (page 8), drinking in the White Barn before catching the train to Manchester for his performances. Jimmy was a comedy actor and writer on radio and television, best known as Pa Glum in *Take it from Here* and as headmaster, "Professor" James Edwards in *Whack-O!*

Jimmy Edwards, outside the Blue Cap.

Another personality who rode with The Hunt was **WILLIAM FREDERICK "BUFFALO BILL" CODY** (1846 - 1917). William Cody was an American scout, bison hunter and showman. He founded Buffalo Bill's Wild West show and in 1883 it toured the United States, Europe and Great Britain. While hunting with the Cheshire Hounds, it is maintained that, being unable to keep his seat in an English saddle, he sent for an American one from Liverpool, where his show was appearing. In 1887 Cody attended a meeting of the hounds at Shipbrook, Davenham, and in 1904 his show visited Northwich. On these occasions he resided at Forest Hill Farm, Sandiway. A post in the stables, adjoining the farm, is said to bear his carved initials.

One of the nine founder members of the Tarporley Hunt Club was George Wilbraham who also came to live in Cuddington but more of him elsewhere (page 93).

William Cody, known as "Buffalo Bill", stayed at Forest Hill Farm when he road with the Tarporley Hunt.

Although only a few of the Masters of the Cheshire Hounds lived in the parish it is the

26 Masters' Hunt Servants and their "whippers-in" and "kennelmen" who made their homes in the cottages at the Forest Kennels, Sandiway, to be near their place of work. Many of them were considered to be at the top of their profession.

JOSEPH "JOE" MAIDEN (1795 - 1864) was the most famous, and according to Gordon Fergusson in his book *The Green Collars*, "the greatest of all Cheshire Huntsmen". He was with the Tarporley Hunt from 1832 until 1844 and served five masters. Joe Maiden had only been at the Kennels for a season when the new kennels were built. Completed in May 1834, a stone plaque was mounted over the feed house which read:

Joseph Maiden, Masters' Hunt Servant.
(Mark Bevan Collection)

These Kennels were built
by the Subscribers
to the Cheshire Hounds
A.D. 1834
Sir Harry Mainwaring, manager
Joseph Maiden, Huntsman
John Douglas, Architect
(This is the father of the more famous John Douglas on page 25).

Born at Linley, Much Wenlock, Shropshire, Joseph Maiden was popular with all the members of the Cheshire Field. Unfortunately, he scalded his leg badly in 1829 which caused him many painful, sleepless nights but it did not keep him out of the saddle. He often hunted six times a week. With his one-eyed "whipper-in", Tom Rance, it is said they were an unlikely but formidable team. Twice he broke the same leg and over the years nine or ten small pieces of bone had to be removed from it. Eventually, long after leaving Sandiway, the limb had to be amputated below the knee, but still it did not stop Joe's hunting. He furnished himself with two new legs, one for walking and one for riding. Joe Maiden's celebrated mount was a fine 16 hands bay called Pevorette. Lord Delamere offered £1,000 (over £70,000) to anyone who could beat Joe Maiden over a four mile course of Cheshire countryside.

Joe had an excellent reputation for looking after his hounds, so in 1842 his despair can only be imagined when he noticed, in a couple of his beloved dogs, coughing and weakness, symptoms of distemper, a highly contagious and dreaded canine disease. Over the next few weeks, one by one, he and his small staff had to drag out and destroy the entire pack of 60 hounds. Then he travelled to Hampshire to replace them at a cost of £400 (£31,600). When Joe Maiden retired he was given the Blue Cap Inn but only stayed as landlord for two years before he was back in Hunt service; this time for the North Staffordshire, where he remained for 19 seasons. On January 1st 1838, Joseph Maiden was presented with a silver fox's mask stirrup cup (hall-marked 1806) by Arthur Wellington Hervey-Aston, and when Joe left Sandiway, he was given another cup and £250 (£22,000) at a dinner at the Blue Cap. Joe Maiden left a wife, Ann, and three children: James, Alfred and Alice.

JOHN "JACK" GODDARD (1849 - 1916) came to the Kennels in 1875 as "whipper-in" and, partly due to his character and determination, there were huge turn outs at most of his meets. In 1886, 400 people, a massive number for those days, hunted at Oulton. Described as "the faithful Jack Goddard" he was a brilliant horseman and was said to have a wonderful voice to listen to when in the field. Jack retired in 1895 after twenty years service. Like Tom Rance, he had never wanted to take over as Huntsman. When he left the Kennels a substantial amount was raised and a cheque presented to him. He went to Davenham, working for some years as a publican and, at his death, left the surprising sum of £5,852 3s 9d (£328.000) to his widow, Ellen Caroline Goddard, which reflected the generosity of his testimonial. Ellen bore him three sons: John, Will and Fred. Jack Goddard was buried at Whitegate and a further £52 (£3,000) was collected towards a tombstone for his grave.

John "Jack" Goddard, "whipper-in", working to keep the hounds in line.

FREDERICK (FRED) CHRISTOPHER CHAMPION (1864 - 1918) was Huntsman from 1903 until 1911. His nephew was Bob Champion Junior, the father of Bob Champion, the celebrated jockey who won the Grand National on his horse, Aldaniti, in 1981, a year after he was told he had testicular cancer. The Bob Champion Cancer Trust has raised millions of pounds for cancer research.

Fred Champion was born and brought up in Kildare, Ireland. Bridger, his first child, was also a native of the Emerald Isle, but Fred's other three children: Fred, Mary and James, were born in Sandiway. All four attended Sandiway School which, at the time, was situated at the fork where Weaverham Road meets School Lane. Seven generations of the Champion family were professional huntsmen. Champion's health began to fail towards the end of his time at the Forest Kennels and he had a fall at Wrenbury, breaking three ribs, but the Duke of Westminster, his Master as the time, remained loyal to Fred, taking him to France with him in 1911. Fred Champion was working for the Staffordshire Hunt when he died in St George's Hospital, London. He bequeathed nearly £4,000 (£250,000) to his wife, Mary.

Fred Champion
(Mark Bevan Collection)

JOHNNY O'SHEA (1938 - 2015) was another Irishman. He touched many people's lives by his invigorating enthusiasm: Prince Charles to name but one. The Prince bought a race horse, "Sandiway Lad", from Johnny, and he and his wife, Ann, were invited to the Prince's marriage to Diana Spencer. In the summer of 1980, the Secretary of the Tarporley Hunt Club wrote to the Prince's Private Secretary offering commiserations to Prince Charles on a painful accident he had endured on the polo field. He added a postscript from O'Shea, the retiring huntsman, hoping His Royal Highness would be well enough for a day with the Cheshire's before the end of the season. When a reply came back from the Private Secretary, the Prince had written on the letter - with his own left hand - "Tell O'Shea it is the only reason I want to get better!!"

An exemplary horseman, Johnny O'Shea was at the Forest Kennels, Sandiway, from 1966 until his retirement in 1991. An invitation day was given for him at Cholmondeley Castle shortly before his retirement on 5th Feb 1991. No less than 14 hunt servants, besides his own three "whippers-in", and an impressive field of 120 from all over the British Isles, turned out to support him. Even his wife, Ann, was in the mounted field, the first time for 32 years, and Prince Charles sent him a special message wishing him well.

Moss Cottage on the Cholmondeley Estate became John Joseph O'Shea's new home where he established himself as a canny greyhound trainer, finding success all over the country. His wife is still living on the Estate. He is father to a son, James, and the late Maureen.

Johnny O'Shea, Huntsman for the Cheshire Hunt, 1966 - 1991.

THE MUST MENTIONS

Although not officially in Cuddington or Sandiway, there are eight large houses only a short distance from the Parish Boundary that were occupied, at one time or another, by some distinguished men and women that it would be remiss not to include within the context of this book. The civil boundaries have altered several times over the years and letters and records reveal that residents often considered themselves to be living in Sandiway.

Sir Aubrey Brocklebank

SIR AUBREY BROCKLEBANK (1873 - 1929) lived at Nunsmere Hall, Oakmere, which was built for him in 1900. Born at The Hollies, Much Woolton, Liverpool, Sir Aubrey was Chairman of the Brocklebank Shipping Line and became an influential Director of Cunard in the 1920s. It was said that at Nunsmere he mused over 7,000 plans and 16 different models before he finally chose the blueprint for the Queen Mary which was launched, five years after his death, in 1934.

John Brocklebank

The Brocklebank line were reputed to be the largest private fleet in the world. They eventually ceased shipbuilding but continued trading with India, China, Antwerp and Japan. Sir Aubrey married Grace Jackson, the youngest daughter of Lord Allerton. When he died at Fitzroy House, Marylebone, he left the tremendous sum of £307,834 (over £17.25m). His son, John, continued to live at Nunsmere and eventually, he too, became chairman of Cunard. When John was forced to retire through ill-health, plans had commenced for the QE2.

Nunsmere Hall today.

CONRADE HENRY COULTHURST (1796 - 1832) lived at Sandiway Cottage, Hartford. His father, Conrade Coulhurst, was heavily into the slave trade with Barbados, but young Conrade had no interest in following in his parent's unhappy footsteps. From childhood he had dreamt of exploring Africa. As the London Gazette for 1832 notes, *"His Eton school books show maps of Africa with his imaginary journeys into its interior and in Barbados* (he worked there as a lawyer after Oxford University) *he took long walks, in the heat of the day, to acclimatise himself to the high temperatures he would have to endure in Africa"*. He wrote long poems about the continent (*Soliloquy of Mungo Park* is one). Conrade was willing to fund the expedition himself but, through his introduction to the Royal Geographical Society, was financed by the Colonial Office, and supplied with valuable scientific instruments and letters of recommendation written in Arabic for

Sandiway Cottage (also named Sandiway House or Sandiway Bank) has been the home of many distinguished people.

"African Princes and Rulers". He sailed on the Agnes, from Liverpool, and made his way to the trading post of Old Calibar, on the Niger Delta, where he hired a canoe, a crew and a guide to take him upriver. However, after a fortnight's travel, the Igbo King refused him transit and Conrad Coulthurst, hugely disappointed, was forced to return to the Agnes where he contracted a fever and died. His main aim had been to follow the course of the Bahrel Abiad River from rise to termination (about 1,200 miles) but, as with other intrepid explorers of the time, he "fell a sacrifice to the enthusiasm for African discovery". A sad end to a lifelong obsession. At the time of his death, the Journal of the Geographical Society said that Mr Coulthurst's powerful descriptions and observations *"must impress every mind with the conviction of the great loss which science has had to deplore in his untimely death"*. Here is an example of his evocative prose in a hasty letter home:

"Nothing can exceed the beauty of the night forest of the Ferdinand Po; the finest trees in England are dwarfs in girth and height in comparison; and its highest peak equals in elevation that of Tenerife... however it is generally mantled in clouds... I much enjoyed bathing in its clear, transparent brooks, where the water is always pure and cool from the shady roof some 100' above; but here I cannot venture, on account of the alligators with which the river swarms... I had an excursion yesterday to Creek Town, once a flowing place, but now almost depopulated from the effect of African witchcraft. I saw remains of handsome French mirrors and English sofas and chairs offered up to the Devil... Every house of any pretensions... has attached to its fetish tree in the centre of the open quadrangle or court, a skull, suspended to avert ill luck from its inmates... but the horrid error of their belief lies in the opinion that when an African gentleman goes to the other world he will be respected in proportion only to the number of slaves and dependants he carries with him; so that the best feelings of our nature are actually enlisted in the perpetration of these wholesale murders but I can attest their treatment of their slaves is milder than I could have imagined...".

In 1899, his sister, Elizabeth Sarah Coulthurst, left a legacy of £500 (£45,000) towards a new church for Sandiway, whilst another sibling, Catherine C. Grey, who married Lord Booth Grey of Vale Royal House, created a Charity for the poor of the "Chapelry of Hartford".

Sir John Fowler Leece Brunner
©National Trust Images

SIR JOHN FOWLER LEECE BRUNNER (1865 - 1929) was another to sojourn at Sandiway Cottage. The son of one of the founders of Brunner Mond, Sir John was a director of his father's company which had a market capitalization of over £18 million (£910m). He was also MP for Northwich (1910-1918) and Southport (1923). During WWI he offered his home for wounded soldiers returning from Belgium and France; promised serving men that he would hold open their jobs at Winnington, and paid their wives full wages. His granddaughter, Katherine, is the present Duchess of Kent. He left the amazing sum of £876,102 (£49.1m) to his son, Felix John Morgan Brunner, Baronet.

LIEUT.COL. RONALD "RONNIE" BOLTON LITTLEDALE (1902 - 1944) was one of only 31 prisoners ever to escape from Colditz. His father, John Bolton Littledale, owned many hundreds of acres of land in the district and on his death, in 1889, left £57,189 (over £5m). The family home was Sandiway Cottage. Ironically, despite his son's amazing escape, and earlier successful bids for freedom, "Ronnie" was killed in September 1944 when his jeep was blown up by a landmine in Normandy.

"Ronnie" Bolton Littledale

Ronald Littledale's WW2 medals were sold in 2011, for £33,000.

SIR THOMAS ALGERNON EARLE (1860 - 1948) was yet another Sandiway Cottage resident. In 1889 he produced a history of his family which contains a wealth of information and is held within the Earle Collection by the National Museums Liverpool: Maritime Archives and Library. Outside St George's Hall, Liverpool, there is a bronze statue of William Earle, the Great Uncle of Sir Thomas and the Earle Baronetcy of Allerton Tower, Woolton, was created in 1869 for another ancestor, businessman Hardman Earle. Several of the Earle dynasty served as Mayors of Liverpool. Sir Thomas Earle managed the company that co-owned and founded the Liverpool to Manchester railway. This was the first public inter-city line. As the passenger terminus for the new line, George Stephenson, in 1836, built Edge Hill, the oldest surviving passenger railway station in the world. Thomas Earle married Edith Leith and at his death, on the on the Isle of White, left £114,040 (£3m).

Sir Thomas Earle

SIR KEITH LILLINGTON NUTTALL (1901 - 1941). On Tarporley Road stands Overdale, a large country house built around 1875. Between the two world wars it was occupied by the heir to the Nuttall civil engineering fortune, Sir Keith L. Nuttall. It was during Sir Keith's time in charge, in the 1920s and 30s, that his firm (Edmund Nuttall, Sons & Co. Ltd.) built the Queensway Tunnel under the river Mersey. It opened in 1932 at a cost to the City of Liverpool and the County Borough of Birkenhead of £7million (£400m). Other major projects completed by the engineering contractors are: The Manchester Ship Canal (1894); The Liver Building in Liverpool (1911); the Dartford Tunnel (1963); the Tyne, Kingsway and Medway Tunnels in

Sir Keith Lillington Nuttall. Photo: ©National Portrait Gallery, London.

Overdale, the home of Sir Keith Nuttall, was originally designed as a "Hunting Box" for the Wilbrahams (page 89).

(1967), (1971) and (1998) respectively, several projects for the 2012 Summer Olympics and, recently, the construction of the Crossrail railway line in London. Sir Keith was killed in action in 1941 and his shares were inherited by his eight-year-old son, Sir Nicholas Nuttall, (1933–2007). Later, as a tax exile in the Bahamas, Sir Nicholas became a passionate campaigner for the protection of the marine environment. His third spouse, Miranda Quarry (he married four times), was the ex-wife of Peter Sellers.

From all accounts, another Overdale resident, **MAJOR CYRIL DEWHURST** (1873 - 1941), was one of Cuddington and Sandiway's most colourful characters. He was the brother of Harry Dewhurst (page 26) and head of Messrs G. & R. Dewhurst, Cotton Manufacturers, Manchester. He was a Major in the Lancashire Hussars, Commander of the 15th Battalion, West Yorkshire Regiment in the 1914-1918 war, and a keen member of the Tarporley Hunt Club. Major Dewhurst had been unfortunate enough to lose a leg and found it necessary to keep four different artificial limbs: for riding, golfing, dancing and bridge. The hunt had a repertoire of hunting songs of which this is one verse:

*"D is for Dewhurst, the wildest of men.
He is fond of his port, his tongue and his pen."*

He owned Conjuror II which his son, Cyril Peter Dewhurst, rode to a creditable third in the Grand National. Cyril Jr emigrated to the Island of Roseau, Dominica, in the West Indies, where he married and had nine children. Major Cyril Dewhurst and his wife, Eleanor Mary Wrigley, had just two: Anthony and Elizabeth. The latter lived in the Northwich area all her life. Major Dewhurst died at Overdale and his effects came to £119,530 (£6m)

John Gustav Jarmay during his time at Brunner Mond.

SIR JOHN GUSTAV JARMAY (1856 - 1944) lived at The Lodge, Hartford (now Whitehall), until about 1914 and then Pettypool House, Whitegate, very close to the Sandiway Parish boundary. Born in Hungary, he became a distinguished director of Brunner Mond & Co. having trained as an industrial chemist before joining the firm, in 1880, to work on the ammonia soda process. After rising rapidly through the ranks, Jarmay was appointed to the board of directors in 1889. He had over forty patents to his name, including ones dealing with the manufacture of soda, soap and glass. Sir John Jarmay was largely responsible for the technical progress of Brunner Mond, as well as a number of other companies with which he was connected. At the outbreak of war, in 1914, Jarmay led the industrial effort required to make sufficient high explosives for the armed forces. In 1918, he was made a Knight Commander of the

Pettypool House over 100 years ago.

British Empire, "in recognition of valuable services rendered during the war in the manufacture of munitions". In 1926 Brunner Mond was absorbed into Imperial Chemical Industries (ICI) and John Gustav Jarmay carried on his career within the company. His wife, Charlotte Wyman, was a very active member of the Red Cross during the First World War, and was made an OBE in 1919. John Gustav Jarmay's demise occurred at Hatfield in Hertfordshire.

Two more of Brunner Mond's elite, who resided at Pettypool at varying times during the first three decades of the 1900s, were **HERBERT ALFRED HUMPHREY** (1868 - 1951) and **GEORGE PATON POLLITT** (1878 - 1964). During their careers both men engaged in chemical research of national importance. The Imperial College of Science, Technology and Medicine hold a whole raft (seven boxes) of papers concerning Herbert Humphrey and George Politt, including correspondence between the two gentlemen when Herbert was Technical Adviser and Chief Engineer at the Ministry of Munitions, Department of Supply, and George was at Brunner Mond, Winnington (1915-17). The letters are relating to experiments to improve the production of high explosives, particularly the manufacture of calcium nitrate and nitrate ammonia for TNT.

George Paton Pollitt

Herbert Alfred Humphrey is also remembered for his invention of the Humphrey Pump (1906) which was capable of pumping 250,000 gallons per hour to a head of 35 feet. It was exhibited at the 1910 Brussels Exhibition where it gained two Grands Prix awards. In 1919 he was appointed Director and Consulting Engineer to Synthetic Ammonia and Nitrates Ltd. From 1926 until 1931 he was again at ICI, as their Consulting Engineer. Herbert became a Fellow of Imperial College in 1932 and in 1939 was awarded the Melchett Medal by the Institute of Fuel. His Publications include, *Papers on large gas engines, gas producers and similar subjects*.

Herbert Alfred Humphrey, inventor of the Humphrey Pump, lived at Pettypool House.

Herbert Humphrey married Jessie Jones in 1891, the same year he became Manager of the Refined Bicarbonate and Crystal Department at Brunner Mond. To start with their home was at Westward House, Dyer Terrace, Winnington, but by the turn of the twentieth century they had moved to Pettypool. The couple divorced in 1916, and the following year Herbert wed Mary Elizabeth Horniblow. He had one son, the bacteriologist John H. Humphrey, with his first wife and two sons and two daughters with Mary. In 1945, Herbert Alfred Humphrey retired to Hermanus, Cape Province, South Africa, where he died in 1951.

The World War I years were busy for George Pollitt. As well as his work for the Admiralty at ICI, he had an illustrious military career, swiftly rising up the ranks to Lieutenant Colonel in the Intelligence Corps, and then the Royal Fusiliers. He commanded a battalion of the Special Brigade (conducting gas operations) on Jan 16th 1916, and in 1918 won a second bar to add to his Distinguished Service Order (DSO), whilst commanding the 11th Lancashire Fusiliers in the German attack on the Aisne. George was wounded and mentioned in despatches four times, especially for his outstanding leadership skills.

On the 12th February 1930, ICI applied to patent an invention, the design of three men, namely, "Henry Brownsdon, Walter Nimmo and Lieutenant Colonel George Paton Pollitt of ICI House, Millbank, London". On the 12th August 1931, Patent Number 354,718 was finally accepted. The invention related to an improved method of tracing the flight of shot from a shotgun cartridge. George Pollitt was a director of Brunner Mond/ICI from 1919-1945. His publications include *A Thesis on the Catalytic Process of the Manufacture of Sulphuric Acid* and in *1942, Britain Can feed herself.* Born in Blackburn and the son of a bank manager, George Pollitt never married but in retirement was to become High Sheriff of Shropshire (1945) whilst living at Harnage Grange, Shrewsbury. He travelled all over the world, including Barbados, Hawaii, West Virginia, Greece, Australia and Pennsylvania, where his brother Gerard Paton Pollitt, was a top dentist. His pastimes were golf, tennis and shooting. He died in Cornwall in 1951.

GEORGE CROSS (1834 - 1896) Five generations of the Cross family tilled the land at Earnslow Grange, Whitegate. George Cross was typical of the area's many gentlemen farmers (Slater's Directory for 1883 gives well over a hundred farms in the district). George owned 170 acres and employed five men to work in the fields and two women for duties in the farmhouse. He left £14,218 (£1.3m).

Earnslow Grange, as it looks today.

ISADOR FRANKENBURG (1845 - 1917) arrived in London from Russian Poland in 1857, and by the mid 1860s had opened a workshop manufacturing leather bags. In 1881 he was living in Salford with his wife, Frances Slazenger Moss (of tennis equipment fame), their eight children (four more were to be added) and his mother, Bertha. By then he was the owner of a leather and India rubber goods business, employing 78 workers. By 1892, Isador Frankenburg owned two factories - The Greengate Rubber and Leather Company, Salford, and the Irwell Rubber Works, in Ordsall Lane, which made rubber for Industrial purposes. By 1914, the former business, now I. Frankenburg and Sons, had a staff of nearly 2,000. Isador was the first Jew to become mayor of a town in

A 1907 advert for Isador Frankenburg's leather factory.

the Manchester area and was credited with bringing peace to the cotton industry following the strike of 1908. He lived the last eight years of his life at Hefferston Grange, Weaverham (page 119) and left the enormous sum of £31.5 million. His son, Ralph, was killed in the wreck of the *SS Berlin,* off the Hook of Holland, in 1907 and Isador gave a painting to the Salford Museum in his memory. Another son, Sydney Solomon Frankenburg, founded the Manchester branch of the British Legion and his wife, Charis Barnett, trained as a midwife and founded the first birth control clinic in Salford. She was also a magistrate, chiefly in the juvenile courts and wrote several books concerning "common sense" with parenting.

THE WARBURTONS were a significant legal family and their paths frequently crossed with those of royalty. Five generations lived at Hefferston Grange. It was with William the Conqueror that the Warburtons first came to Britain, in the guise of one, Odard, who was the grandfather of Adam de Dutton. Adam had three sons and Sir Geoffrey, the youngest, settled in Great Budworth. In the reign of Edward I, Sir Peter Dutton, on coming into the possession of the township of Warburton, assumed the name for himself and during the reign of Henry VII the family came to Arley.

Sir Piers Warburton of Arley, the father of Peter Warburton of Hefferston Grange.

The first of the Warburtons to live at Hefferston was Peter, the third son of Sir Piers Warburton of Arley and his wife Elizabeth, daughter and heiress of Richard de Winnington. Peter married Alice Cooper and they had six children including three sons. The first, Peter, married Magdalin Moulson, daughter of Sir Thomas Moulson, Lord Mayor of London (1634) and the auditor to the Exchequer of Queen Elizabeth. The second, William, wed one of the Brooke daughters from Norton Priory and, the third, Sir Richard Warburton, married Anne Vavasour, a lady in waiting to Queen Elizabeth I. Anne attended the queen's funeral and received a pension of £66 13s. 4d. (£16,000) from King James. She is not to be confused with a courtier of the same name who had several affairs with aristocratic gentlemen, at least two illegitimate children, for which she was imprisoned in the Tower of London, and fined for bigamy. This promiscuous lady was thought to be Anne's aunt. Sir Richard Warburton trained as a lawyer at Lincoln's Inn, and from 1592 until his death was one of *The Honourable Band of Gentlemen Pensioners*, a bodyguard to the British Monarch. In 1601, he was elected Member of Parliament for Bridport and, after receiving a knighthood in 1603, was elected MP for Penryn where he sat until his death in 1610.

Hefferston Grange was built in 1741 for Philip Henry Warburton, incorporating parts of an earlier house dating from about 1700 but replacing the earlier medieval structure.

Peter and Magdalin inherited Hefferston Grange and they produced eight offspring, but it was their first born, another Peter, who is worthy of note. As well as being Tory MP for Chester (1647), Peter Warburton was a distinguished barrister and judge. At Oxford, where he matriculated from Brasenose College, Peter graduated with a BA on 22nd November 1606. On 27th January 1607 he was admitted as a student at Lincoln's Inn, where he was called to the bar in 1612. Parliament appointed him on 22nd February 1647 as justice of the court of sessions for Cheshire, Flintshire, Montgomeryshire and Denbighshire, and advanced him on 12th June 1649 to a judgeship in the Court of Common Pleas. On 14th March 1655 he was placed with Sir George Booth and Sir William Brereton on the militia commission for Cheshire. Soon afterwards he was transferred from the court of common pleas to the upper bench. He died in 1666, and was buried in Fetcham, Surrey.

Matthew Henry (1662 - 1714) was a nonconformist minister and Bible commentator who founded a Presbyterian chapel in Chester in 1700. His writings are still published today. He was the father of Philip Henry Warburton the last owner of Hefferston. Photo:©National Portrait Gallery, London

Mary Philpot, Philip Henry Warburton's niece, and the wife of Nicholas Ashton - see page 5.

Described as "That learned and religious gentleman... Judge Warburton of Helperston", Peter was also an ardent non-conformist. He insisted that his motto - "Christ is the Christians' all" - be put up in every room at Hefferston Grange and engraved on rings given out at his funeral. George Moss, in his delightful book, *Village of Moonbeams*, says that in case Peter should run into difficulties for his unorthodox religious beliefs, a brick escape tunnel leading to the cellars was built, which is still there today.

Judge Peter and Alice had twelve children. One of the dozen, Robert, also had a large family but it was his daughter, Mary, who provided the necessary heir. Mary married the Rev'd Matthew Henry whose family were on intimate terms with the royals. His grandfather, Philip, had been near in age to Charles and James, the two princes, and they were often at the Henry's house in the early years and Philip visited the royal household. Philip Henry was present at the execution of his chum, Charles I, and is said to have heard "such a groan as I never heard before and desire never to hear again". James II came to Chester in 1687 and Matthew was one of the persons to meet the king, after all he was the son of James' old playmate Philip.

The Stables, formerly the old stable block to Hefferston Grange, and now a modern link-detached property. It is thought that the building retains the original clock tower and oak beams.

Matthew's wife, Mary Warburton, inherited Hefferston when her brother Peter died unmarried in 1727, and when Mary died, in 1731, the estate was inherited by her son, Philip Henry, who then took the Warburton surname. Philip Henry Warburton was not as pious as his father, living as squire of Hefferston until 1760 when he died, unmarried. In 1763 the Grange became the property of Mary Philpot, the daughter of Philip's sister, Elizabeth, as a dowry upon her marriage to Nicholas Ashton (page 5). In the meantime there was further royal approval for the family when The Warburton Baronetcy, of Arley, was created on 27th June 1660 by Charles II for George Warburton, of Arley Hall, whose great-uncle was none other than Judge Peter Warburton of Hefferston Grange.

ROBERT HEATH (1816 - 1907) lived at Hefferston Grange from the time of his marriage to Ann, who was a mere 23, to his 55 years, until his death at the age of 92. He was a farmer with 260 acres, twelve farm workers and six house staff. When he died, at 92, his wife and children: Beatrice, Nina and Robina, were still relatively young but he left them well provided for to the sum of £40,281 (£4.4m).

In 1893 **CAPTAIN WILLIAM ("WILL" or "WILLIE") HIGSON** (1863 - 1942) succeeded his father, **JOHN HIGSON** (1817 - 1893), to Oakmere Hall, only a few strides outside Sandiway. John was the first to live in this impressive Victorian mansion. The Higson family owned several highly profitable sugar refining houses in Liverpool and in the 1861 and 1871 censuses, John's brother, William, is described as a "beer merchant". It was their father, Daniel Higson (1830-1914), who founded the famous Higson's Brewery in the city. Captain Willie Higson was joint Master of the Tarporley Hunt and had been hunting in Cheshire since he was seven. He was also a keen polo player and played for his regiment, the IV Hussars for seven seasons. William Higson's brother, **JOHN HAYES HIGSON** (1866 - 1934), took up residence in Oakmere Hall after him. John Higson left £453,788 (£50m) and, his son, William Higson, £638,296 (over £25m). Wealthy men indeed!

A page from the *Sports and Pastimes* magazine for January 1914 showing Captain "Willie" Higson in his hunting garb and his signature.

Oakmere Hall in the time of the Higson family. In all they inhabited the house from the 1870s until the 1920s.

CHARLES JAMES LAMB (1881 - 1942) was the last private owner of Oakmere Hall, living there until about 1939. He was a shipping merchant, operating under the name Coddington and Lamb at 35, St Peter Street, Manchester. There are records of their steamers, in 1917, transporting valuable cargoes of cotton, textiles, perfumery, nails and other goods. The company was dissolved in 1923 by mutual consent. Charles Lamb was born in Egremont, Cheshire, and grew up in Birkenhead. In 1915, he and his wife, Florence May Killey, were living in New York but he died in the UK leaving £132,000 (£6m).

ALEXANDER "ALEX" GEORGE SOUTHCOMBE (1936 - 2016), a retired chemist, lived in an apartment at Oakmere Hall until his recent death on 9th January 2016. During his retirement he invented the Ocean Wave-Master, which could generate an unlimited supply of electricity using sea waves which would dramatically reduce our reliance on fossil fuels and nuclear energy. The invention won the North West Environment Business Award and was a runner-up for the United Utilities low-carbon prize. Extensive studies at the University of Manchester Institute of Science and Technology also concluded the invention to be technically and commercially viable. The Wave-Master was patented in 2000 and a 16-metre prototype was trialled at the New and Renewable Research Energy Centre. During the £1,000 a day trial, the Wave-master did indeed produce electricity. In all forty million pounds was needed to make Alexander Southcombe's dream come true but he passed away before that could come to fruition. He and his wife, Elizabeth Young Southcombe, had two children, Anne and John.

Alexander "Alex" Southcombe

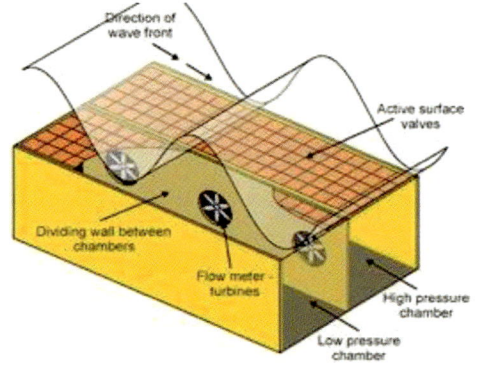

This diagram of the Ocean Wavemaster shows how it would work. The cuboid structure comprises two linked chambers, one maintained at high pressure under the waves, the other at low pressure. The flow of water, due to the pressure differentials, through lines of valves along the top of the structure, can be harnessed through turbines to produce electricity.

Mrs Edith May Pretty (née Dempster)
©National Trust/Angus Wainwright

MRS EDITH MAY PRETTY (NÉE DEMPSTER) (1878 - 1942) gained international fame as the lady who gave the nation the greatest Saxon haul ever found, after the discovery, on her land, of a 27 metre-long Anglo-Saxon burial ship, with all its treasures. For 19 years she lived at Vale Royal, "The Great House" at Whitegate, with her parents, Robert and Elizabeth (née Brunson) and her sister, Elizabeth. The estate, which her father leased from Lord Delamere, extended to almost 5,000 acres and included 86 farms and small holdings, 70 cottages, and industrial buildings extending well into Sandiway and the surrounding villages. Robert Dempster employed 25 indoor staff and the gardens were looked after by 18 gardeners. This was country house life on the grandest scale and Edith was a classic Edwardian society lady - well-educated, articulate and public spirited. The sisters were sent to Roedean boarding school, in Hove, Sussex, followed by finishing school in Paris.

From a young age Edith Dempster travelled across Europe with her family. An interest in archaeology was fuelled by her Uncle, the famous Egyptologist, Professor Archibald Sayce, who frequently holidayed with them. On these jaunts Edith was never far from excavations. As luck would have it, alongside Vale Royal, covered by moss and grass, were the foundations of the enormous Abbey church, which Robert Dempster, at huge personal expense, excavated in 1911-12 with Edith, fascinated by the whole procedure, constantly at his side. The Cistercian Abbey, which the excavations showed to be the largest in the country, was discovered to have been around 400 feet long with 13 radiating chapels. *Vale Royal* (Frank Latham, 1993) records Mrs Mary Hopkirk, Edith's niece, writing that Edith and her father found "the stone coffins of the monks" which they "...filled rather incongruously, with geraniums".

Mary Hopkirk's memoirs also give an interesting insight into another side of Edith's life in Vale Royal. Her Aunt's personal sitting room was on the ground floor, "a huge, cold room looking north and west (the south windows having been blocked) crammed with her immense collection of bibelots (small, decorative ornaments or trinkets) from all over the world. It was

Vale Royal in the time of Edith Dempster. Her father, Robert Dempster, rented the house (1907 to 1925) from Hugh Cholmondeley, 3rd Baron Delamere.

about a quarter of a mile from the bedrooms and quite out of hearing of anyone and, as she used to sit there alone after everyone else had gone to bed, my father gave her a revolver which she kept in a drawer in her desk...". In The Great War, Edith Dempster served as a Red Cross nurse in England and France. She twice raced in her Uncle John Dempster's yacht, Vol-au-Vent, in the Kaiser Cup, which he won in 1903. She was a strong sailor, never prone to sea sickness.

Edith's marriage at Vale Royal in 1926.

It is said that from the age of 18, a certain Col. Frank Pretty, on each of her birthdays, asked for her hand in marriage, but her father did not approve and it was not until after his death in 1925 that Edith felt able to accept Frank's proposal and marry at the age of 42. Robert Dempster, with his huge wealth and standing, had hoped his daughter would marry into the aristocracy. After all, he was the immensely wealthy owner of the Manchester engineering firm of R. & J. Dempster, whilst Frank was merely the son of a modestly prosperous Ipswich corset maker. At her Father's death she and her sister inherited his fortune of £518,819 (£28m).

As their new home together Edith and Frank decided to buy Sutton Hoo Estate, Woodbridge, Suffolk. The marriage was a happy one and in 1930, when Edith was 47 years old, a son was born. They named him Robert, after her father, but four years later, at the age of 56, Frank fell ill and died. Edith was desolate and would sit alone in the house, gazing for hours at the earthen burial mounds close by.

By the summer of 1938, she had decided that the mounds should be investigated and asked the advice of Ipswich Museum. They put her in touch with Basil Brown, a local amateur archaeologist. The first mounds he tackled revealed little, except that each of them had been dug out and robbed centuries earlier. During the winter the dig was suspended, but in the spring of 1939 he began work on the biggest of the mounds, uncovering an Anglo-Saxon ship and its treasure. Heavyweight archaeologists from Cambridge and the British Museum turned up with their trowels and tried to elbow Brown aside but, according to Elizabeth, her sister, Edith, was adamant that if Basil didn't stay, they couldn't dig there anymore. It was her land so they had to agree. The dig yielded gold and silver jewellery, bits of a helmet and shield, a sceptre and a large silver dish. The house safe was too small to keep it all in and, for one night, Edith slept with the remainder under her bed. After Ipswich Museum prematurely announced the discovery, reporters attempted to access the site, so Mrs Pretty paid for two policemen to guard the site 24 hours a day.

The 27 metre-long Anglo-Saxon ship, unearthed on Edith Pretty's land at Sutton Hoo in 1939.

An inquest held in the parish hall concluded that the artefacts were treasure trove, and the lawful owner was Edith Pretty. She decided to donate the finds to the British Museum. A grateful nation's offer to make her a Dame of the British Empire was graciously declined and, this time, her sister's comment was, "That's my favourite thing about Edith, she was so humble".

Sutton Hoo House, now Tranmer House, is open to the public and visitors are encouraged to sit at the table in the window, or lounge in the easy chairs, leafing through magazines published at the time of the dig. Edith's portrait (page 123) gazes serenely down upon the drawing room. She died in Richmond, in 1942, leaving £398,976 (£18.1m).

LADY MARY CHOLMONDELEY (1562/63 - 1625) There can be few other Tudor woman in Cheshire who made such an impact on their contemporaries as Lady Mary Cholmondeley of Vale Royal Abbey. She was described by William Webb, co-author of *The Vale Royal of England*, first published by Daniel King in 1656, as "a lady of great possessions, and for her wisdom, virtue and great hospitality, deserveth worthy remembrance" and by James I as the "bolde lady of Cheshire". It is said that in 1588, Elizabeth the first, knighted Mary's husband Sir Hugh Cholmondeley and Lady Mary, for "her valour and patriotism", a royal act without parallel.

Lady Mary Cholmondeley

Lady Mary was born Mary Holford, to Christopher Holford and Elizabeth Mainwaring of Holford Hall, Plumley, and christened on 20th January 1563. She married first, Sir Randall Brereton of Malpas who died around 1581, and second Sir Hugh Cholmondeley with whom she had eight children: Robert, Hatton, Hugh, Thomas, Francis, Mary, Lettice, and Frances. Sir Hugh passed away in 1601 and in 1616 Lady Mary Cholmondeley left Holford and bought Vale Royal Abbey and its surrounding land which included "...extensive gardens and orchards, six granges (Conewardsley, Bradford, Darnhall, Earnslow (page 118), Knight's, Hefferston (page 119) and Merton), dovecotes, meadow, pasture, heath and moor, all belonging to the late, dissolved monastery."

In the succeeding year she entertained James I, at Vale Royal, for four days and three nights. The King's visit is commemorated on panels in the Royal Bedchamber at Vale Royal House. He went stag-hunting in Delamere Forest with Sir John Done, the Chief Forester, and bestowed knighthoods on two of Lady Mary's sons. Some days later King James wrote to his hostess offering to advance the pair's political careers if they came to court in London. It is

Holford Hall, built for Lady Mary after the death of her husband in 1601. Just a section of the manor house can be seen today.

when she firmly refused his offer that he is alleged to have dubbed her the "bolde lady ". Whether this refusal was the source of the king's statement is conjecture. It could equally have been the fact that she had been involved in a forty-year-long dispute over her father's Holford estate. Christopher Holford died on 27th January 1581. His half-brother, George Holford of Newborough, was the next male-heir, but Mary challenged his legal claim to the land. Finally, around 1620, they came to a settlement, under which Mary Cholmondeley received Holford, and George, the manor of Iscoyd in Flintshire. It appears that Mary was satisfied with the outcome and was soon busy renovating and enlarging her newly acquired inheritance, adding a lath and plaster wing in 1625. For twenty years she also sued the same Uncle over who should have the most important pew in Lower Peover Church (the papers are still preserved there).

In the same year that she entertained King James, Lady Mary Cholmondeley broke her leg which never really healed and she died, at Vale Royal, on 15th August 1625, at the age of sixty-three. She was buried the next day in St Oswald's Church, Malpas. Thomas Cholmondeley, Lady Mary's third son, was the founder of the Vale Royal family who lived in the house until 1907 when it was rented out to the Dempsters (page 123). His descendant, also

Thomas Cholmondeley, was on intimate terms with George IV who created him Lord Delamere in 1821. The fourth Lord Delamere lived with his family at Vale Royal, up to the 1930s.

These alabaster effigies of Lady Mary Cholmondeley and her second husband, Sir Hugh Cholmondeley, are to be found in Malpas church.

The painting to the right, *The Cholmondeley Sisters,* is traditionally said to depict Lady Mary's daughters, Lettice and Mary, who gave birth on the same day. Now in the Tate Gallery, London, it was known to be in the collection of Thomas Cholmondeley, the fourth son of Lady Mary. The babies are swaddled in traditional, red christening robes.
©Tate, London. 2016.

WILLIAM HALL WALKER, 1ST BARON WAVERTREE, (1856 - 1933) was a British businessman, politician, art collector and an important figure in the breeding of thoroughbred racehorses. In 1916 he founded the National Stud, in County Kildare, and served as MP for Widnes for 19 years until he was created Baron Wavertree of Delamere, in 1919. His racing stables were at Sandy Brow, Delamere, where he was living in 1923. In 1928 he purchased a good deal of the Vale Royal Estate but not Vale Royal House which belonged to the third Lord Delamere. Whether he lived in "The Great House" is uncertain but entirely possible.

William Hall Walker was the younger son of Sir Andrew Barclay Walker, 1st Baronet, and his wife Eliza Reid of Limekilns, Fife. He was a wealthy brewer, born in Ayrshire, who moved to live in Gateacre, Liverpool, when he expanded the business.

Lord Wavertree
Photo: ©National Portrait Gallery, London.

As a racehorse owner his most memorable victory was that of The Soarer in the 1896 Grand National, but he is best remembered as a racehorse breeder. In 1900, William Walker purchased the lands around Tully, County Kildare, where he established a highly successful stud farm which led to the breeding of such horses as the 1906 Epsom Derby winner, Minoru. In 1916, William gifted his entire bloodstock to the British government with the idea of creating a National Stud. In the event the stud farm in Ireland became the basis for both the Irish National Stud and The National Stud of the United Kingdom, now located at Newmarket. Wavertree House at the National Stud and its Wavertree Charitable Trust is named in Walker's memory. Currently, the Irish National Stud property consists of 958 acres and is home to some of Ireland's leading stallions. In 1999, the *Racing Post* ranked Lord Wavertree at number 24 on its list of *Top 100 Makers of 20th Century Horse Racing*. Between 1906 and 1910, William Walker created a Japanese garden at Tully which is acclaimed as the finest of its kind in Europe and today is a major tourist attraction.

William's father donated the Walker Art Gallery to the city of Liverpool, and in 1933 Lord Wavertree bequeathed the Gallery a sizeable portion of his paintings collection plus £20,000 (£1.25m) to help the museum with its renovations. In addition, he gifted some of his own sporting works of art to The National Stud which are on display at Wavertree House.

William Hall Walker was Conservative Member of Parliament for Widnes from 1900 until resigning in August 1919. On 27 October 1919 he was raised to the peerage as Baron Wavertree of Delamere, in the County of Chester. On his death, in 1933, the barony became extinct. In his honour, the Lord Wavertree Cup is offered by the English Football Association and his widow, a direct descendent of the playwright Richard Brinsley Sheridan, sponsored lawn tennis tournaments and offered the International Tennis Federation a trophy that was initiated as the Davis Cup. At his death Lord Wavertree was worth £838,290 (nearly £53m)!

My sincerest apologies to those village residents, past and present, who should have been in this book.

This watercolour of Cuddington and Sandiway's famous landmark, the Round Tower, was discovered by Northwich Auction, in a house clearance in Barnton, in 2015. It was painted by T. Yarwood who was said to have painted the scene many times. Another hangs in the lounge at Sandiway Manor Care Home (page 52).